India's External Sector Reforms

India's External Sector Reforms

Vyuptakesh Sharan
Indra Nath Mukherji

OXFORD
UNIVERSITY PRESS

OXFORD
UNIVERSITY PRESS

YMCA Library Building, Jai Singh Road, New Delhi 110001

Oxford University Press is a department of the University of Oxford. It
furthers the University's objective of excellence in research, scholarship, and
education by publishing worldwide in

Oxford   New York

Athens   Auckland   Bangkok   Bogota   Buenos Aires   Calcutta
Cape Town   Chennai   Dar es Salaam   Delhi   Florence   Hong Kong   Istanbul
Karachi   Kuala Lumpur   Madrid   Melbourne   Mexico City   Mumbai
Nairobi   Paris   Sao Paolo   Shanghai   Singapore   Taipei   Tokyo   Toronto   Warsaw

with associated companies in   Berlin   Ibadan
Oxford is a registered trade mark of Oxford University Press
in the UK and in certain other countries

Published in India
By Oxford University Press, New Delhi

ISBN 019 565516 8

Typeset in Book Antiqua 10.6 on 12 by Inosoft Systems, Delhi 110 092
Printed at Roopak Printer, NOIDA, UP
Published by Manzar Khan, Oxford University Press
YMCA Library Building, Jai Singh Road, New Delhi 110 001

Preface

In mid-1991, the Indian Government initiated macroeconomic reforms and structural adjustments in different areas of the economy. Reforms in the external sector were of utmost significance since this sector was badly distressed at the time with serious deleterious effects on the pace of economic development. The book analyses the impact of reform measures on the health of the external sector.

We have long been involved with the research of international economic issues, in general, and India's external sector problems, in particular. In view of a fast changing world scenario, we decided to write a book that would acquaint the general reader, with the evolving issues and latest developments. We do realize that a period spanning only about eight years is not sufficient to assess the full-fledged impact of economic reforms. Yet, we are sure, the trends that have been witnessed so far would be indicative of the efficacy of reform measures in curing the external sector of its many maladies.

It would be amiss not to express our thanks to the officials of the Foreign Investment Promotion Board and Indian Investment Centre, Government of India, who have provided us valuable data. We are also thankful to our family members for their support. However, for the analysis and interpretation of data, we assume the entire responsibility.

VYUPTAKESH SHARAN
INDRA NATH MUKHERJI

Contents

List of Tables   ix

1. INTRODUCTION   1
   Concept of Economic Reform   2
   Key Economic Reforms Introduced in India   5

2. PRE-REFORM SCENARIO   13
   First Two Decades of Planning   13
   Period of Revival   15
   Worsening Trend in the 1980s   17
   Crisis of the Early 1990s   19
   Reasons for Ailing Balance for Payments   22

3. REFORMING FOREIGN TRADE   26
   Measures of Foreign-trade Policy Reform   26
   Impact of the Reforms   30
   Conclusion   43

4. FOREIGN DIRECT INVESTMENT   44
   Measures of FDI Policy Reform   44
   Impact of the Reforms   47
   Conclusion   59

5. ATTRACTING NRI INVESTMENT   61
   Modes of NRI Investment   62
   Impact of the Reforms   66
   Conclusion   75

6. FOREIGN PORTFOLIO INVESTMENT   76
   Channels for the Flow of FPI   76

Reasons for Choosing FPI 77
Measures of FPI Policy Reform 78
Magnitude of Investment 81
Conclusion 86

7. INDIA'S OVERSEAS INVESTMENT 88

Rationale behind the Internationalization 88
of Indian Firms
Measures of Overseas Investment Policy 92
Reform
Size and Pattern of Overseas Investment 94
Foreign-exchange Earnings due to Overseas 102
Investment
Conclusion 104

8. EXTERNAL INDEBTEDNESS 114

Concept of External Debt 114
India's External Debt Burden during the 116
Early 1990s
Measures of Policy Reform to Cure 118
External Indebtedness
Impact of the Reforms 119
Conclusion 126

9. AN OVERVIEW 127

Pre-reform Scenario 127
The Policy Package 128
Impact of the Reforms 131
Conclusion 134

10. RECENT TRENDS 137

External Trade 137
Foreign Direct Investment 139
Foreign Portfolio Investment 140
Non-resident Indians 141
Overseas Investment 141
External Debt 143
BOP at a Glance 143
Moving Closer to CAC 144

Appendix: A Note on Capital-account Convertibility 145

Bibliography 154

Tables

2.1. Current Account Transactions 16
2.2. Some Capital Account Transactions and
Foreign Exchange Reserves 20
3.1. Growth in India's Foreign Trade 33
3.2. India's Major Export Markets 40
3.3. Product Pattern of India's Export 41
3.4. India's Terms of Trade 42
4.1. Size of FDI 49
4.2. Major Country-wise FDI Approvals in India 52
4.3. Sectoral Pattern of FDI Approvals 55
4.4. Sectoral Pattern of Actual FDI Inflow 57
4.5. Equity-range-wise Distribution of FDI Cases 59
5.1. Direct Investment Approval for NRIs 68
5.2. Actual Flow of Direct Investment of NRIs
in Different Sectors 70
5.3. Portfolio Investment Approval 71
5.4. NRI Deposit with Non-banking Companies 72
5.5. Bank Deposits by NRIs 74
6.1. Euro-issues: Approval and Actual Flow 83
6.2. Foreign Portfolio Investment 87
7.1. Geographic Pattern of India's Overseas Ventures 98
7.2. Sectoral Pattern of India's Overseas Ventures 100
7.3. Foreign Exchange Earnings of India's Overseas
Ventures 103
A 7.1. Country-wise/sector-wise Distribution of
WOSs abroad 105

A 7.2. Country-wise/sector-wise Non-WOSs Ventures
        Abroad   109
  8.1. India's External Indebtedness   120
  8.2. India's External Debt: Government and
        Non-government Components   122
  8.3. India's External Debt Service Payments   124
  8.4. External Debt Indicators of Highly Indebted   126
        Countries
  9.1. An Overview of India's Balance of Payments   135
        Position

1

Introduction

One of the most significant developments in the world economy since the 1980s has been structural adjustments and macro-economic reforms introduced by a number of developing countries. India has not been an exception. Trends towards liberalization in the Indian economy were well apparent during 1980s, but took concrete shape in mid-1991 when the economic conditions of the country, especially in the external sector, turned unmanageable. The Indian government had no option but to resort to full-fledged macroeconomic reform and structural adjustment in order to bring the economy back on rails.

Economic reforms initiated in India during mid-1991 were broad-based and comprehensive. They embraced vital sectors of the economy and consequently, the policies—industrial, fiscal, monetary, financial and external—underwent sea-change. The reforms in different sectors are interlinked, though the way they are related may not always be direct and proximate. Since the present study is confined to the reforms in the external sector, it is devoted to the policy changes in the field of both current account and capital account transactions, more especially foreign trade, foreign investment inflow, external debt, and the country's overseas investment. Our objective is not merely to delineate major policy changes, but more importantly, to assess whether their impact has been positive. It is a fact that some of the policy changes have long-term implications and therefore it would be unfair to evaluate their impact within a short span of eight years or so. But, at the same time, there are policy changes that do have short-term implications and their impact on the external sector is already visible. After a brief explanation of the concept of economic reforms and the broad strategy adopted for their implementation in India, the subsequent chapters present the health of the external sector on the eve of launching of reforms followed by a discussion of performance of this sector during the period of reform. The concluding pages of the volume put together our overall analyses and inferences evaluative of the reform process.

Concept of Economic Reform

Motivations behind Economic Reform

At the very outset, it would be pertinent to explain the circumstances that led to economic reform in a large number of developing countries. Going through the pages of history, we find that the immediate post-War world economy witnessed large-scale decolonization, following which there was an intense desire for development among then newly independent countries. Influenced by the 'big-push' theory then gaining acceptance, these countries raised the quantum of investment through greater mobilization of domestic resources and external support. There was a common belief that the gains from growth would automatically trickle down to the lowest rung of the social ladder. But in many countries, growth rate remained very low despite huge investment. In some others, inspite of a high growth rate, millions continued to live below poverty line. In fact, structural weaknesses or defective macroeconomic policies came in way of the very process of growth and of equitable distribution of the gains from it.

Apart from the structural weaknesses on the domestic front, developing countries had to face severe external shock (Balassa, 1981). The soaring international oil prices of 1973–4 and 1979 gave a jolt to the balance of payments position of the net oil-importing developing countries. The current account deficit of these countries jumped up from $ 8.3 billion in 1970 to $ 39.6 billion in 1975 and to $ 43.1 billion in 1979

(The World Bank, 1980). All this hampered the process of economic development. The efforts of over three decades failed to pull the developing world out of stagnation.

This state of affairs — structural weaknesses on the domestic front as well as the external shock — was responsible for motivating policy-makers to adopt structural adjustment and macroeconomic reform. In May 1979, Robert McNamara, the then President of the World Bank indicated this course of action at the Manila meeting of the United Nations Conference on Trade and Development (UNCTAD). Again, at the annual meet of the International Monetary Fund (IMF) and the World Bank in September 1979, he outlined the structural adjustment lending strategy. The World Bank took the lead and the IMF began making available funds for macroeconomic reforms in the subsequent period.

Objectives of Economic Reform

The process of economic reform or economic adjustment combines macroeconomic reforms and structural adjustment and aims at ensuring better allocation of resources, thereby improving economic performance through changes in economic policies. Macroeconomic adjustment involves an immediate change in policies and aims at achieving short-term objectives. Structural adjustment, on the other hand, involves more fundamental changes in the way the economy operates. It modifies the very structure of the economy towards meeting long-term objectives. It takes into account reordering of priorities and reconsideration of policy instruments. There may be variations across different countries adopting economic adjustment, but by and large the policy package encompasses production, saving and investment, sectoral development, monetary and budgetary targets and the external sector (Woodward, 1992).

Despite differences, macroeconomic stabilization programme and structural adjustment, overlap each other. For instance, depreciation of currency by the orders of the monetary authority is a structural reform insofar as it encourages a shift of production towards internationally tradable goods. But, at the same time, it is considered a part of macroeconomic adjustment inasmuch as its immediate aim is to reduce demand for imports in order to reduce trade deficit. In fact, the structural adjustment process cannot go on in an environment of macroeconomic instability. Macro-economic adjustment is linked with the process of structural adjustment at two levels—one at the beginning, when a healthy macroeconomic environment is needed, and the other after the structural adjustment process is over and changes in key variables are called for (Rodriguez, 1989).

The main purpose of a macroeconomic adjustment programme is to reduce a country's need for external finance through improvement in balance of payments, and to keep inflation at a low and manageable level. This concept rests on the theory of international monetarism which postulates that deterioration in balance of payments and a rise in inflation are both symptoms of excessive money supply. It thus calls for a tight credit and monetary policy, cutting of budgetary deficits and rationalizing inflationary financing. All this helps lower the demand in the economy and hence reduce import. The goods previously demanded at home are released for export. Consequently the balance of payments improves.

The improvement in the balance of payments can also be brought about through depreciation of currency that cuts the demand for imports and raises exports by making them more competitive in the international market. In a long-term framework, it makes the production of exports and import-substitutes more profitable thus improving the balance of payments.

Structural adjustment programmes are more wide-ranging. The major objectives are to reduce the role of the State in matters relating to the private sector, to allow prices and income to respond freely to market forces, and to open the economy to foreign trade and investment. The rationale behind reducing the role of the public sector is that private sector operations are comparatively more efficient and that private markets encourage an optimal allocation of resources. This is particularly true in many low-income countries where the role of the State has grown far beyond its capacity. Again, the proceeds of privatization represent a non-inflationary source of financing for the budgetary deficits. To achieve it, government expenditure as a percentage of national income is reduced, production and provision of services is shifted from the public to the private sector, and unnecessary governmental interference is removed from the private sector.

Similarly, the structural adjustment process believes in the market forces and attempts to bring prices in line with the market conditions — administered prices are done away with. This in turn calls for removal or reduction of subsidies and price control, and the introduction of, or increase in, user's charges for public services.

Last but not least, opening of the economy to foreign trade and investment improves the performance of the economy in the sense that free access to imports and the discipline of foreign competition help improve the efficiency of domestic production. Foreign investment alleviates pressure on the balance of payments and bridges the technology gap. Structural adjustments involve relaxation, or removal, of restrictions on foreign trade and investment.

Key Economic Reforms Introduced in India

The strategy of reform introduced in India in July 1991 presents a mixture of macroeconomic stabilization and structural adjustment; or in other words, it is guided by both the short-term and the long-term objectives. In view of the policy-makers, 'stabilization was necessary in the short-run to restore balance of payments equilibrium and to control inflation... (although) the reform measures (were) equally important in the medium-term if the economy was to grow and become competitive in the world' (GOI, 1993). From this viewpoint, a number of reform measures have been introduced in different sectors of the economy. The important ones are mentioned hereunder.

Fiscal Reform

Let us begin with fiscal reforms that were emphasized in view of the high rate of inflation and seriously distressed balance of payments in the early 1990s. The basics of economics tell us, that greater the fiscal deficit, larger is the government borrowing from the Reserve Bank of India (RBI). The greater the amount of borrowing, the larger is the money supply and higher is the rate of inflation. Similarly, fiscal deficit is closely linked with the worsening of the balance of payments. Expansion in aggregate money supply and aggregate demand results in higher import demand. On the other hand, inflation and thereby increased cost of production reduces the competitiveness of exports resulting in a trade deficit. Fiscal deficit also leads to greater external borrowings and sometimes, commercial borrowings when official development assistance is not available to the required levels. Consequently, servicing of the debt burden becomes increasingly difficult. The outflow of foreign exchange has a deleterious effect upon the balance of payments.

The statistics show that fiscal deficit during FY 1990–1 was as large as 8.4 per cent of GDP. It was over twice the level of mid-1970s and over one and a half times the 1981–2 level (GOI, 1993). Naturally, the aim of fiscal reform was to correct the fiscal imbalances. It envisaged a reduction in fiscal deficit initially by two percentage points. This was to be achieved through containment of government expenditure and augmentation of revenues, curbing conspicuous consumption and reversing the downward trend in the share of direct taxes to total tax revenue. The initial steps were in the direction of reduction of fertilizer subsidy, abolition of cash compensatory support for exports, abolition of subsidy on sugar and disinvestment of a part of the government's equity holding in select public sector undertakings. The Government accepted in 1991–2 almost all the major recommendations of the Tax Reforms Committee headed by Raja Chelliah and implemented most of them subsequently. The purpose was to raise revenue through better compliance in case of income tax, excise and customs as well as to make the tax structure stable and transparent.

Monetary and Financial Sector Reform

Measures to contain the growth in money supply were taken through both fiscal and monetary disciplines. To this end, quarterly targets for RBI credit to the central government were set along with targets for bank credit to government. Monetary reform aimed at doing away with interest rate distortions and rationalizing the structure of lending rates. In the pre-reform period, government borrowing was done at administered interest rates while the lending rates for the commercial sector were high. The new policy attempted to apply market-related rates to government borrowings, an appropriate example of which was the 364-day treasury bill. Besides this, it tried to reduce the number of lending rates which were as many as six at the time of launching of the reforms. Initially, they were reduced to three with the ultimate aim of reducing them to only two—one being the general rate, and the other being concessional for the weaker sections of society.

The monetary policy reforms went for reduction in statutory liquidity ratio (SLR) and the cash reserve ratio (CRR) in line with the recommendations of the Narsimham Committee Report of 1991. During mid-1991, SLR and CRR were very high. High SLR helped mobilize greater resources for the central and the state budgets, while high CRR helped check the expansionary effect of the budget deficit on money supply. But since they pre-empted a sizeable portion of banks' resources and diverted them to low-income earning assets, profitability of banks was badly affected. To ensure profitability, banks had to raise interest rates on lending to the commercial sector that created further problems. In view of this, SLR was to be cut down in stages over a three-year period from 38.5 per cent to 25 per cent. The CRR was to be axed to a level below 10 per cent over four years.

Besides the above, the new policy tried in many ways to make the banking system more efficient. It brought in greater competition among the three constituents of the banking system—public sector banks, private sector banks and the foreign banks, and attempted to eliminate administrative constraints. The branch licensing policy was liberalized to help rationalize the existing branch network. Banks got freedom to relocate branches, open specialized branches and set up controlling offices. Special tribunals for recovery of loans were set up. Guidelines were issued for opening new private sector banks with the idea of making them more viable. New accounting norms regarding classification of assets and provisions for bad debt were introduced in tune with the Narsimham Committee Report. The banks were expected to meet capital adequacy norms at par with the international standard under which they have to maintain unimpaired minimum capital at least equal to 8 per cent of the total of risk-weighted assets and other off-balance-sheet exposures. In case capital of the banks was found inadequate, additional capital was to be mobilized from the capital market in form of new equity, or in other words, through the disinvestment of government holdings in the capital structure.

Reforms were not limited to the banking sector alone. They permeated to the capital market as well. An element of liberalization was introduced into the system through the repealing of the Capital Issues (Control) Act, 1947 and abolishing the office of the Controller of Capital Issues. With this, companies no longer needed government approval for approaching the capital market. The companies issuing securities were free to fix price and premium. The reforms went on to permit companies to approach the international capital market through the issue of Euro-equities under the global depository receipt (GDR)/American Depository Receipt (ADR) mechanism.

However, reins were not loosened completely—sufficient care was taken to check malpractices. The Securities and Exchange Board of India (SEBI), which had been set up in 1988 to regulate the capital market, was given statutory powers to rationalize stock exchange. This institution took a number of steps to increase transparency in the system with a view to promoting healthy practices, speedier transactions, and ensuring improved services and greater protection to investors. Some additional steps were the inspection of mutual funds and stock exchanges, registration of intermediaries, disclosure of material facts by security-issuing companies, adherence to code of conduct by the merchant bankers, permission to foreign institutional investors (FIIs) and foreign brokers to operate in the capital market.

Industrial Policy Reforms

The industrial policy reforms stressed the removal of major hurdles in the way of industrial production, making this sector internationally competitive in terms of price and quality. For this purpose delicensing was introduced on a significant scale, except for a few industries of strategic importance. Delicensing, however, necessitated filing of an information memorandum with the government while setting up or expanding an industrial unit.

The new industrial policy removed most of the restrictions that had been imposed on the inflow of foreign technology and investment through the amendment to the Foreign Exchange Regulation Act (FERA) in 1973. The ceiling on foreign equity participation was raised to 51 per cent in normal cases and even up to 100 per cent in special cases. Provision was made for automatic approval of foreign collaborations where the foreign equity participation was limited to 51 per cent of the total equity. Besides this, the area of operations of foreign investors was widened to cover trading and services, power, oil production, and refining and marketing. Automatic approval was also given to technology agreements in high-priority industries and those involving a lump-sum payment of up to Rs 10 million and a royalty payment of up to 5 per cent of the domestic sales and 8 per cent of exports.

The policy-makers realized that the Monopolies and Restrictive Trade Practices Act was a major hurdle in the way of industrial production as big industrial houses were not allowed to set up new units in many fields. Though the Act has been abolished in the interests of industrial development, there is a commission to control unfair trade practices.

Last but not least, the new policy reinterpreted the role of public sector units in a way that is relevant to present needs of the economy. Despite the fact that the public sector units have had a role to play in fostering growth and preventing concentration of wealth, a host of accompanying problems ultimately told on their productivity and some units were even rendered sick. The new policy took all these facts into account and provided a few guidelines. First, eleven out of seventeen industries reserved for the public sector were thrown open to the private sector. Secondly, the policy encouraged dis-investment of government holdings in the equity share capital of public sector enterprises. This was initially in favour of mutual funds and other institutions, but later, in favour of public in general. Thirdly, the public sector units were provided greater autonomy of management that could be helpful for generating reasonable profits. This was to be achieved through a system of Memorandum of Understanding (MOU) which provided for an agreement between the enterprise and the concerned Ministry for minimising governmental interference, but at the same time making the enterprise accountable to the government at the year end. Fourthly, the new policy showed concern for the revival of sick units. It brought public sector units under the ambit of the already existing Sick Industrial Companies (Special Provision) Act, 1985 and the Board for Industrial and Financial Reconstruction (BIFR). The Sick Industrial Companies Act was further amended in December 1993 to facilitate early detection of sickness in companies and speedy enforcement of remedial measures on the basis of the recommendations of the Omkar Goswami Committee in the months preceding December 1993. As per the provisions, sickness was to be reported to the BIFR that in turn was to recommend the closure of the non-viable units and for the revival of the viable units. The interest of the retrenched workers was to be protected through assistance from the National Renewal Fund.

External Sector Reform

The external sector reforms is our main area of concern and so a detailed discussion follows in the subsequent chapters. Nevertheless, a brief mention of the broad strategy may be made here to complete the overview of economic reform policies in India. It may be noted that the policy reforms touched upon every aspect of the balance of payments problem.

Most significantly, the exchange rate was rationalized. The rupee was depreciated to remove maladjustment between the real and the nominal exchange rates. The depreciation of the rupee was followed by its convertibility on current account. First, it was made partially convertible, and then after a year it was made fully convertible mainly on trade account. By mid-1994, the rupee was made fully convertible on all current account transactions. The rationalization of process also included a shift to the system of a managed floating exchange rate. All the above steps aimed at encouraging foreign-exchange earnings.

Imports were liberalized to boost production. Tariff was axed with a view to arresting the cost of production within meaningful limits. These were accompanied by various export promotion measures. In case of invisibles, the strategy was to limit the inflow of external loans, particularly non-concessional loans, so that interest payments remained within manageable limits and then gradually began to shrink, improving the net earnings from invisibles. Moreover, over-seas operations of Indian companies were encouraged to give a boost to investment income. Thus, through restructuring trade and exchange rate and encouraging the invisible earnings, the new policy aimed at reducing current account deficit.

The IMF was approached in 1991-2 to meet the deficit and resolve the immediate crisis. However, from the medium and long-term points of view, the new policy stressed on foreign investment rather than external assistance. Servicing external debt had been one of the key factors behind the balance of payments crisis.

The area for the operations of foreign investors was widened as also their stake in the Indian enterprises increased through raising the ceiling on their participation in equity capital. Automatic approval of foreign collaboration agreements in certain cases was added encouragement for inflow of foreign direct investment. Besides foreign direct investment, portfolio equity investment from abroad was also given an impetus. Foreign institutional investors were allowed to operate in the Indian capital market and Indian companies were allowed to raise capital in the international capital market. All this represented a big move towards opening the economy. One more milestone was set by moving towards capital account convertibility based on the strategies outlined by the Tarapore Committee (June 1997), but in view of the lack of sustainability of the economy, the monetary authorities have followed a policy of go-slow on this count.

This in brief, is the process by which economic adjustment was initiated in different sectors of the economy. The evaluation of the success of the strategy would be an interesting study. Since the present analysis is confined to the external sector reforms, subsequent chapters are devoted to the appraisal of the reform process in foreign trade, foreign investment, India's joint-ventures abroad, and external debt.

2

Pre-reform Scenario

For any evaluation of reform measures in the external sector, it is imperative to have a fair idea of the state this sector was in in the pre-reform era. Although emphasis is on the period immediately preceding the reforms, it would be appropriate to have an overview of the external sector through the first forty years of planning.

First Two Decades of Planning

Current Account Scenario

The First Plan (1951–6) presented rather a cosy picture. The low volume of imports was largely financed through exports. Moreover, net invisible earnings compensated for nearly three-quarters of the trade deficit. On the contrary, the Second Plan period (1956–61) witnessed large imports owing to stress on infrastructural industrialization. Export earnings did not meet even two-third of the import bill. Invisible earnings met barely 13–14 per cent of the trade deficit. The annual average of deficit on current account inflated to $ 822 million as compared to $ 63 million during the First Plan period (see Table 2.1).

In view of rising deficit on the current account, the Indian Government decided to encourage export by providing export incentives during the Third Plan period. Though these yielded good results, the import bill was too large to be disbursed through export earnings. Again, net invisible earnings turned negative on account of servicing of foreign loans. The annual average of deficit on current account rose to $ 1074 million.

The Indian Government devalued the rupee in the first week of June 1966 while withdrawing some of the export incentives. But the immediate impact of devaluation on the growth of export was very little as the price elasticity of demand for Indian products in the international market was found to be low. At the same time, the net invisible earnings yielded a negative figure of a higher magnitude. As a result, the annual average current account deficit was as big as $ 1105 million during 1966-9.

Meeting the Current Account Deficit

Up to mid-1950s, the Indian Government, as admitted by the then Minister of Finance, was not very receptive to external assistance (The Statesman, 14 December 1955). Nevertheless, the current account deficit was met entirely by external assistance and that too on fairly lenient terms.

In the following quinquennium, a large number of donors emerged on the map of the global economy perhaps due to the emergence of the Cold War (Ohlin, 1966; 1966a). The quantum of aid inflow increased. But since the magnitude of current account deficit was large, the net aid inflow covered only 70 per cent of such deficit. The rest of the deficit was met either through borrowings from the IMF or through drawing down of the foreign exchange reserves. The foreign exchange reserves were depleted rather drastically from $ 1648 million at the end of the First Plan period to $ 390 million at the end of the Second Plan period.

In the Third Plan period (1961-6), aid availability was still larger. The net aid inflow was sufficient to cover the current account deficit — foreign exchange reserves were thus, comparatively stable during this period. The three Annual Plans of 1966-9 were not very different. Net aid inflow met around 98 per cent of current account deficit — drawings from the IMF were additional. Consequently, the foreign exchange reserves augmented marginally (see Table 2.2).

Period of Revival

Shrinking Deficit

The last year of the Fourth Plan (1969–74) coincided with the first oil shock that raised the country's import bill phenomenally. But India could bear the burden because by then, the positive results of devaluation had begun to show. Moreover, some of the export incentives were restored and the growth rate of export rendered higher than that of imports — the trade deficit narrowed. The net earnings from invisibles were still negative, nevertheless, the annual average current account deficit during the Fourth Plan period was lower at $ 557 million. This was almost half the 1966–9 level.

Improvement in the current account balance continued through the Fifth Plan period and showed surplus for the first time in decades. In fact, economic boom in the oil-exporting nations raised demand for Indian products pushing up the growth rate of exports (Chisti and Upadhyay, 1981). Again, invisible trade played a supportive role. The Indian construction industry secured contracts worth millions of dollars in the oil-exporting countries that made a positive contribution to investment income. This also expanded employment opportunities — the Indian migrants remitted a part of their income to their families back home. Positive net invisible earnings resulted and the annual average balance of current account showed a surplus of $ 291 million (see Table 2.1).

Capital Account Transactions

The size of net aid inflow was smaller during the Fourth Plan either on account of larger amortization or due to lower gross disbursements. But the management of the external sector was not difficult because, firstly, the size of current account deficit was not large, and secondly, there were Special Drawing Rights (SDRs) allocations and drawings amounting to $ 31.8 million.

In the first two years of the Fifth Plan (1974–9), the Government had to raise resources from the IMF, but that was

Table 2.1 Current Account Transactions

Annual average in $ millions

Plan period	Import	Export	Trade balance	Net Invisible Earnings				Current account balance
				Overall	Interest	Remittances	Travel	
First	1533	1306	-228	165	N.A.	N.A.	N.A.	-63
Second	2242	1287	-956	134	-27	N.A.	N.A.	-822
Third	2533	1569	-964	-110	-142	70	9	-1074
1966-9	2579	1677	-902	-202	-227	85	-16	-1105
Fourth	2682	2271	-411	-145	-278	145	28	-557
Fifth	6305	5520	-786	1077	-276	821	394	291
1979-80	11822	7656	-4166	3220	-346	1953	1108	-946
Sixth	15600	9264	-6336	3754	-672	3363	1122	-2582
Seventh	20579	12748	-7831	2012	-1892	2453	940	-5819
1990-1	27915	18477	-9438	-242	-2763	2069	1064	-9680

Note: Figures do not tally because of rounding off.
Source: V. Sharan (1994), 'Trends in India's Balance of Payments', *Journal of Social and Economic Studies*, XI, pp. 39–59.

a short-term arrangement. Overall, the current account was buoyant; and so, whatever accrued as net inflow of aid, augmented the foreign exchange reserves. The reserves shot up from $ 736 million at the end of 1973–4 to $ 6421 million at the end of 1978–9. Here, it would not be irrelevant to mention that from the 1950s to the 1970s, the role of foreign direct investment in bridging the current account deficit was only minimal. It is a fact that in the wake of the foreign exchange crisis of late 1950s, the Indian government encouraged foreign investment in the country, but in many cases, it was technical collaboration involving no inflow of foreign exchange. Financial collaborations did represent foreign exchange inflow, but in most of the cases, they did not entail investment in cash. Capital goods were supplied by foreign investors (that too at an inflated price) in lieu of their participation in the equity of the Indian company (Sharan, 1968).

In 1968, the foreign investment policy turned somewhat restrictive narrowing the options for entry of foreign capital. An amendment to the FERA in 1973, dealt a harsh blow on foreign investment inflow. The permissible areas for foreign investment were narrowed; and the ceiling on foreign equity participation lowered to 40 per cent. Foreign branches were to be Indianized through sale or amalgamation. Foreign equity participation in Indian companies was to be contained at 40 per cent through dilution of shares. Naturally, foreign investors did not relish this and their investments fell abysmally. Those not ready to mould themselves to the changed conditions dismantled their operations in India leading to disinvestment and outflow of foreign exchange (Encarnation, 1989).

Worsening Trend in the 1980s

Rising Deficit

Happiness with respect to the current account came to an abrupt end with the second oil shock in 1979. The bigger import bill widened the trade deficit. Unlike the first oil shock the overall export performance after the second oil shock was depressed on account of recession in the industrialized countries. Further, the net invisible earnings declined, mainly as a result of growing interest payment on foreign loans. The annual average current account deficit was as large as $ 2582 million during the Sixth Plan period (1980–5).

The Seventh Plan (1985–90) commenced at a time when current account deficit had achieved a new high. The Government made a move towards outward-looking policy. It liberalized imports and provided incentives for export. Exports and imports, both rose at a higher rate. The stagnancy in domestic oil production and huge food imports in the wake of the drought of 1987–8 stepped-up the imports further. All this inflated the trade deficit to an unprecedented level.

What was more disturbing is that the net invisible earnings shrank continually—from around three billion dollars in 1985–6 to slightly over half a billion dollars in 1989–90—primarily on account of swollen interest payments on external loans which had doubled during this period. If one delves deeper, it is found that a couple of factors were responsible for huge interest payments. The first was the increasing share of hard-term loans by the International Bank for Reconstruction and Development (IBRD) in the overall World Bank assistance to India. Secondly, it was the large ratio of fiscal deficit that compelled the Government to borrow more from abroad. In the absence of desired concessional assistance, the Government had to resort to commercial borrowings that involved higher rates of interest.

In other words, the huge trade deficit accompanied by declining net earnings on invisible account pushed up the current account deficit to $ 5819 million annually during the Seventh Plan period which was almost two-and-a-quarter times larger than in the Sixth Plan period. In 1988–9 alone, it amounted to $ 7996 million which was 2.9 per cent of GDP as compared to 1.8 per cent during the late 1950s through mid-1970s and (–) 0.6 per cent during the latter half of 1970s (Jalan, 1991).

Structural Changes in Capital Account

Statistics show that during the 1980s, external assistance failed to play the decisive role in bridging the current account deficit it had played during earlier decades. This was primarily because of large amortization that had squeezed the magnitude of net aid inflow. The Government approached the IMF for SDR 5 billion assistance under the Extended Fund Facility during the early 1980s although the actual amount drawn was only SDR 3.9 billion.

The structural change in capital account transactions during the 1980s was also manifested in the form of growing foreign direct investment, for which the policy of the Indian Government was found encouraging. The amount of foreign investment inflow was significant, yet in view of the exorbitantly large current account deficit, the inflow did not reach even the half-way mark. The natural victim was the foreign-exchange reserves that were ultimately not capable of meeting even two-and-a-half months' import bill (see Table 2.2).

Crisis of the Early 1990s

Unprecedented Deficit

The balance of payments crisis of the 1980s worsened by the early 1990s. During FY 1990–1, the trade deficit broke all previous records, amounting to $ 9438 million. There were a host of factors that were responsible for such a huge trade deficit. The invasion of Kuwait by Iraq on 2 August 1990 brought sharp imbalances in the trade structure. India had to look for substitute sources for oil import in place of Iraq and Kuwait. Moreover, since the contracts for crude oil and products were market-related, the average price of crude oil paid by India rose from $ 15 per barrel during April–July 1990 to $ 30 during the following August–November. The price of petroleum products rose from $ 182 per tonne to $ 354 per tonne during the same period. Consequently, India's oil import bill soared from $ 3.8 billion in FY 1989–90 to $ 5.9 billion during the following fiscal year. Taking into account the other imports, the bill stood at $ 27.9 billion, 35.7 per cent higher than the average of the preceding quinquennium. On the other hand, India's export to West Asia dropped by an

Table 2.2 Some Capital Account Transactions and Foreign Exchange Reserves

Annual average in US $ millions

Plan period	External assistance		IMF transactions			Private account (net)	Foreign currency assets at the end of the period
	Gross inflow	Amortization	Drawings	SDR allocation	Repurchases		
First	93	-21	-	-	-17	-9	1648
Second	605	-27	40	-	-18	-11	390
Third	1179	-140	103	-	-71	-15	383
1966-9	1320	-696	278	-	-193	-58	526
Fourth	1034	-339	15	66	-74	-13	736
Fifth	1639	-447	170	31	-185	Neg.	6421
1979-80	1844	-660	-	156	-103	-27	6324
Sixth	1890	-773	1050	31	-49	438	5482
Seventh	2843	-2268	-	-	-722	2546	3368
1990-1	3397	-4383	1858	-	-644	2426	2236

Note: Neg. stands for negligible.
Source: V. Sharan (1994), 'Trends in India's Balance of Payments', *Journal of Social and Economic Studies*, XI, pp. 39–59.

estimated $ 280 million. It was also difficult to realize the export proceeds from the warring countries and hence a sum of $ 114 million came to a dead account (GOI, 1993).

Exports also languished on account of recessionary trends in industrialized countries, and more particularly in those countries that were large importers of Indian goods. The growth rate of real gross national product in the US fell from an average of 3.1 per cent during 1981–9 to barely 1.0 per cent in 1990 and to (–) 0.5 per cent in 1991. The expansionary forces in Germany and Japan lost momentum increasingly during the late 1980s and in 1991 (Inter-Economics, 1992). India's export to the East European countries was marred by economic and political upheaval in those countries. It grew simply by 1.6 per cent in dollar terms during FY 1990–1 as compared to 42.7 per cent in the preceding fiscal year (GOI, 1992). Again, the movement in the exchange rate, which was supportive to India's export during the 1980s, ceased to be so. Most importantly, there was a fall in the unit value realization in case of a number of export commodities. The import compression measures implemented in the late 1990s did contain growth in imports, but entailed upon industrial production, and thereby on export.

Besides strains on the trade account, invisible earnings also came under acute pressure. Table 2.1 shows that the net invisible earnings that were positive and covered a part of the trade deficit during the preceding one-and-a-half decades, turned negative during FY 1990–1. This was mainly due to the fall in remittances on account of several non-resident Indians (NRIs) returning to the country during the Gulf War. In addition, there was a large amount of outflow of foreign exchange on the investment income account. The current account deficit attained a new high of $ 9680 million, 3.3 per cent of GDP.

Financing of Deficit

Financing such a huge deficit was not an easy task, particularly when the low credit-rating of the Indian economy in the international capital market had weekened the prospect for the external loans and other forms of inflow and when the amortization ratio was abnormally high. Authorization of external loans during FY 1990-1 was $ 4236 million as compared to $ 6070 million in the preceding fiscal year and $ 8877 million during FY 1988-9. The NRI deposits both in rupee and foreign currency accounts sagged to $ 140 million from a level of $ 1245 million in 1989-90. The amortization ratio was so high that there was a net outflow of resources to the tune of $ 533 million with respect to commercial borrowings. On the whole, a high ratio of amortization at 94 per cent squeezed the net disbursements to $ 207 million. Taking into account the amortization of rupee debt, the net disbursements were rather negative by $ 986 million.

The foreign direct investment also faced a downward trend due to the low credit-rating of the economy. This was an important factor behind the fall in the net inflow of resources on private capital account from $ 3113 million in 1989-90 to $ 2426 million in 1990-1. The Indian Government had to approach the IMF. It made use of its reserve tranche and the first credit tranche and borrowed under the Compensatory and Contingency Financing Facility — all taken together totaled to $ 1858 million. Foreign exchange reserves were drastically axed. Consequently, they dropped to $ 2236 million by March 1991. Any substantial drawing from foreign exchange reserves was not possible at this stage. The Government had to sell gold to the Bank of England with a buy-back option but this did not have a lasting effect. Foreign exchange reserves dipped further to $ 1156 million by May 1991, an amount capable of financing only about a three-week import bill. The crisis was unprecedented.

Reasons for Ailing Balance of Payments

Except for the first half of the 1950s and the latter half of the 1970s, India's external sector continued to remain under strain. The strain, however, varied in intensity and nature during different segments of the pre-reform period. The magnitude of the current account deficit during the 1980s and the early 1990s was quite enormous as compared to that till the early 1970s. The capital-account inflows on official account fell far short of requirements during the 1980s and early 1990s. As a consequence, large drawings were made from the IMF to meet the requirements. Net inflow on the private capital account solved the problem to some extent.

There were many factors behind the ailing balance of payments, a few significant ones are mentioned here. In a growing economy, the growth in imports is a normal phenomenon. What strained India's balance of payments was that it had to face three oil shocks since the early 1970s. In the pre-Green Revolution period, there was shortage of food-grains during most years which had to be imported. During the post-Green Revolution period, it was the import of fertilizers that strained the trade balance. Government policy was also responsible for growth in imports. The inward-looking strategy of industrialization raised imports of capital goods and components with a view to expansion of pro-duction of import-competing items. This policy changed during the 1980s in favour of outward-looking strategy. Imports were liberalized especially since 1985, but its immediate impact was manifest in growing imports. Import liberalization stabilizes import but only in the long run. Its immediate impact is often not favourable, particularly when there is already a balance of payments crisis. This was not only the Indian experience but was found in many other countries, such as Tanzania, Ghana, Sri Lanka, and Argentina (Taylor, 1988).

The rising imports would not have been a cause for concern, had export earnings been sufficient to finance them. A number of incentives were provided to boost export, but the inward-oriented policy structure till the 1970s arrested any sizeable growth in export. The reason was that the domestic market remained protected behind high tariffs. The domestic market was more profitable than the export market. The study of the World Bank and the Industrial Credit and Investment Corporation of India (ICICI) shows that even after taking into account various export incentives, export profitability remained lower than domestic profitability. Firms preferred the domestic market and exported only when there was a surplus available after domestic sale. Moreover, the domestic industrial structure lost competitiveness due to continued protection both with respect to quality and price (Rangarajan, 1990). Besides, the tight import policy entailed upon industrial production and export. Naturally, when the import policy was made liberal during the 1980s, industrial production grew rapidly and exports grew faster.

It is evident that till the 1970s, external assistance was available to the capital account in sufficient quantity and at concessional interest rates. The magnitude of interest payment rose continually with an increase in external debt and squeezed the net invisible earnings, and simultaneously put pressure on the capital account through repayment of the principal. Nevertheless, the net aid available could meet the current account deficit. However, during the 1980s, the availability of official aid could not be expanded to the extent of the current account deficit. The Government was compelled to commercially borrow. Moreover, the growing fiscal deficit was another factor behind the growing inflow of commercial borrowing. The harder terms lessened the net fund availability and pushed up the external debt.

The problem with the external loans forced the Government to approach the IMF. Here it was confronted with a ceiling on getting funds from different facilities. Conditionality in the use of funds was yet another problem. Moreover, the external debt including the IMF borrowing turned so huge during the late 1980s that the debt/export ratio was comparable with the value of such ratio in 17 heavily-indebted countries of Asia, Africa and Latin America (The World Bank, 1990).

Foreign direct investment (FDI) played a role to some extent in meeting the current account deficit during the 1980s and early 1990s. However, if such investments took place in order to reap the advantage of the protected market in India, their impact was always questionable (Jalan, 1991). It is difficult to quantify or analyze such motivated investments, in the absence of payments made on account of dividend, royalty, technical fees, and payments to foreign technicians in foreign exchange. Studies have shown such payments exceeded the inflow of investment. It is also found that imports necessitated by foreign-controlled rupee companies exceeded the value of exports generated by them (Sharan, 1992). Last but not least, foreign investors are fair-weather friends — when the balance of payments crisis had been serious during the early 1990s, there was a large-scale disinvestment by NRIs. FDI in general dropped. Thus the overall picture of India's external sector was not a very comfortable one during the pre-reform period and especially at the time of launching the reforms.

3

Reforming Foreign Trade

Reforming foreign trade was the first step in the process of India's external sector reform. This step was very significant in the sense that the size of the trade deficit during the fiscal year 1990–1 was abnormally large amounting to over $ 9.4 billion, amounting to 3.2 per cent of GDP (GOI, 1999). The policy package came to be an essentially outward-oriented one. It aimed at augmenting export for which necessary changes were brought about in the very approach towards import and in the exchange rate policy. The present chapter outlines the broad policy measures and examines how far these measures have proved effective in improving trade performance.

Measures of Foreign-trade Policy Reform

The redesigning of foreign-trade policy covers quite a broad area and a variety of measures. Over the period of reform, some new measures have been added to, and a few of them have been withdrawn from, the policy package from time to time, depending upon the changing performance and position of this sector. The measures that have been taken in this regard can be grouped under four broad heads:

- rationalization of exchange rate policy
- liberalization of imports
- incentives to exporters
- simplification of procedural formalities and fostering of transparency

Rationalization of Exchange Rate Policy

In the very first week of July 1991, the rupee was depreciated by around 20 per cent vis-à-vis a basket of five currencies, viz. the US dollar, the Deutschmark, the British pound, the French franc and the Japanese yen. The purpose was to bridge the gap between the real and the nominal exchange rates that had emerged on account of rising inflation and thereby to make exports competitive. In March 1992, the Liberalized Exchange Rate Management System (LERMS) was introduced. It provided for a dual exchange rate system under which 40 per cent of the export proceeds were to be surrendered at the official exchange rate and the remaining 60 per cent were to be converted at market-determined rates. The units in the export-processing zones (EPZs), 100 per cent export-oriented units (EOUs) and the units in the electronics technology park were allowed to convert their entire foreign exchange earnings at market rate. The system was further liberalized in March 1993 when full convertibility was introduced implying that the entire export proceeds were convertible at market-determined exchange rates. By August 1994, the entire current account earnings came to be convertible at market rates.

The unification of the exchange rate in March 1993 was an added step. The rupee came to be on managed float implying that its value is determined by the forces of supply and demand, although the Reserve Bank possesses the right to intervene in the market to stabilize the exchange rate. The monetary policy announced from time to time takes care of stabilization in the value of rupee. The RBI has often gone for intervention selling and purchasing US dollars so that the value of rupee could be stable.

Liberalization of Imports

The reform measures seek to arrest trade deficit not through massive import restrictions but through export expansion for which import liberalization is a pre-requisite. Initially, automaticity was injected into the process of import by introducing a freely tradable instrument, known as Eximscrip. This provided import entitlement up to a certain percentage of export value. But with the introduction of LERMS, the provision of Eximscrip was withdrawn. Under LERMS, capital goods and intermediates came to be imported freely subject to normal tariff and availability of foreign exchange from the free market.

Since 1992-3, tariff rates were gradually cut with the result that the peak tariff rates dipped from a level of over 300 per cent during the pre-reform period to 40 per cent within a few years. For a couple of years, this percentage was subject to a surcharge of 5 per cent which in effect raised the peak tariff rates to 45 per cent. But the Budget proposals for 1999-2000 discontinued the surcharge with the result that it came down to 40 per cent again. The import of capital goods witnessed a preferential rate. In this case, the import-weighted custom duty rates came down from 97 per cent in 1990-1 to 30 per cent in 1998-9 (World Bank, 1998). The Export Promotion Capital Goods scheme provides for duty-free imports of capital goods. A number of sectors, such as agriculture and allied sectors, industries manufacturing electronic items, gems and jewellery, sport and leather goods, toys, food-processing industry, specified bio-technologies and small-scale engineering industries have been enjoying the benefits of this scheme. There is threshold limit for this privilege but that has gradually been reduced to a present limit of Rs 10 million. Again, as a member of the World Trade Organization (WTO), the Indian Government has bound about two-thirds of its tariff lines and has been making a phased reduction in these bound levels that will be complete by the year 2005. The Budget proposals for 1999-2000 have taken back some commodities from the zero-duty scheme, but taking into account the non-applicability of special additional duty in these cases, the tariff continues to remain only nominàl. Thus the overall picture shows lower tariff implying lower cost of production and enhanced export competitiveness.

Apart from tariff cuts, quantitative restrictions have been removed from the import of many items, especially capital goods and intermediates. The Indian Government has submitted a detailed proposal to the WTO for curbing quantitative restrictions. It has unilaterally removed quantitative restrictions on imports of around 2300 items from

SAARC countries. Moreover, there is delicensing of large number of imports. The negative list of imports has been pruned sizeably. On the other hand, the open general licence (OGL) list has been broadened. The April 1998 Exim Policy alone delicensed 340 items of import by moving them out from restricted list to OGL list. Many imports previously made through specified public sector agencies stand decanalized.

The system of advance licencing has further liberalized imports. The Exim Policy of 1997-2002 abolishes value-based advance licence scheme, but the quantity-based advance licence scheme continues. The Exim Policy of April 1998 simplifies further the provisions of advance licences. Special import licence is another chain in this series. Certain categories of exporters get them. Many items have been added to this list. For the electronic sector, the entitlement has been raised under this scheme.

Encouragement to Exporters

The reform measures strengthen the channels of export. In this context, EPZs (export processing zones), EOUs (100 per cent export oriented units), export houses, trading houses and star trading houses have got a number of incentives. They get a special import licence and tax holiday for a ten-year period and also get 100 per cent foreign equity participation. The EOU scheme is extended to agriculture and allied activities and trading. The Exim Policy of 1997-2002 allows EOU/EPZ units in agriculture and allied sectors to sell half their production in domestic tariff area. The Government has now permitted the setting up of private software technology parks.

The export policy has sizeably pruned the negative list of exports. In fact, this list is based on strategic considerations, environmental and ecological grounds and on the grounds of essential domestic requirements and socio-cultural heritage.

The reform measures ensure easy availability of export credits both in domestic and the foreign currencies. Their interest rates have been reduced. The Budget proposals for 1999-2000 have provided for credits to exporters at internationally competitive rates to enable them to compete in the international market. The export under all export promotion schemes is exempted from the applicability of 4 per cent special additional duty (SAD). SAD is taken into account for establishing duty drawback rates. The exporters get the facility of forfaiting. With strengthening of foreign exchange reserves, the exporters are now permitted to retain up to 50 per cent of their foreign exchange receipts in an account designated as Exchange Earners' Foreign Currency (EEFC) account. This is as high as 100 per cent in case of the EPZ units and EOUs. This facility protects exporters from inconveniences relating to conversion cost while making payments for imports.

Simplification of Procedural Formalities and Fostering of Transparency

The reform measures have ensured transparency and simplified procedures from the very beginning. The trade and customs classification stands greatly harmonized. The number of duty rates has been gradually reduced to only five. The processes are computerized so as to ensure speedy disposal of applications. Legal requirements have been eased. Now the manufacture-exporters with good record are permitted to furnish a legal undertaking instead of bank guarantees against import of duty-free raw material. The Exim Policy of 1997-2002 represents not only a micro-management approach for specific commodities but also a macro-management approach making the entire scenario quite liberal. The Exim Policy announced in April 1998 provides for automatic issue of advance licences on the basis of information furnished by importers. Moreover, the licensing functions are being decentralized to make them more smooth. Presently, the Ministry of Commerce is contemplating integrating all export promotional schemes into one so as to ensure greater transparency and reduction in transaction costs related to foreign trade licensing, tax procedures and the banking system.

Impact of the Reforms

Some of the measures have started bearing fruit while others have not done so far. Moreover, there are some short-run trends that may not be in conformity with the long-term objectives. For instance, the import liberalization process inflates the import bill in the short run, although in a long-term perspective, import has to stabilize. From this point of view, a period spanning over about eight years may not be sufficient for analysing the impact of reform measures. Nevertheless, this kind of study is expected to unravel some distinctive features that may be useful for future course of action. The present study concentrates on examining:

- whether the size of export has grown and the balance of trade has improved
- whether India has been able to penetrate more into the international market
- whether the export market has diversified
- whether the commodity concentration has reduced
- whether the terms of trade have gone in India's favour and
- whether export earnings have become more stable

Size and Balance of Trade

The normal expectation from the reformed trade policy is that liberal imports will no doubt inflate the import bill, but it will make exports more competitive and will do away with the supply constraints on them. With such a trend, export earnings are expected to gradually finance a greater part of import bill. The size of trade deficit should squeeze in the sequel.

Table 3.1 presents a comparative view of export and import and the resulting balance of trade. The monthly average of import bill surged up by 10.3 per cent during July 1991–March 1992. This rate was lower than that for export. Thus, the monthly average trade deficit was smaller during the first nine months of reform than during the quarter preceding reform.

In 1992-3, the growth rate of export lagged behind that of import. It was 3.8 per cent for export as compared to 12.6 per cent for import. Trade deficit was larger by over two-fold. In fact, it was the recessionary trend in some of the industrialized countries accompanied by political and economic upheaval in the East European countries that had arrested export. During 1993-4, export fared better. Its growth rate was 20 per cent as compared to 6.5 per cent for imports. Trade deficit squeezed to barely one billion dollars which was less than one-third of that during the preceding fiscal year. In the following two fiscal years, the growth rate in export was almost maintained, but import grew at a higher rate with the result that trade deficit grew to $ 2.3 billion in 1994-5 and to $ 4.9 billion in 1995-6. In fact, it was the increased buoyancy in the industrial sector that led to greater imports during 1994-6.

The foreign trade scenario has been quite different since 1996-7. The growth rate in export has turned out not only meagre but has also been on a continual decline. As compared to 20.8 per cent in 1995-6, it was barely 5.3 per cent in 1996-7, 4.6 per cent in 1997-8 and (-) 3.9 per cent in 1998-9. It is a fact that the growth rate in imports too came down significantly during these years — from 28 per cent in 1995-6 to only 6.7 per cent in 1996-7, 6 per cent in 1997-8 and 0.9 per cent in 1998-9 — probably on account of slow-down of industrial activities in the country and drop in oil-import bill. But since the growth rate in export was lower than that of import, the trade deficit went on increasing from $ 5.7 billion in 1996-7 to $ 6.5 billion in 1997-8 and to $ 8.2 billion during 1998-9. The growing trade deficit is evident in the continously declining share of exports in the total import bill. Export earnings that had financed as large as 95 per cent and 92 per cent of the import bill in 1993-4 and 1994-5 respectively, accounted for only 80 per cent of the import bill during 1998-9. Trade balance (on balance of payments basis), which was (-) 1.5 per cent of GDP in 1993-4, moved to (-) 3.9 per cent of GDP in 1997-8 (GOI, 1999). The negativity dropped marginally in 1998-9 in view of slower growth rate in imports, yet the trade balance as percentage of GDP was (-) 3.2 (RBI, 1999). These figures and ratios are very close to those during the period immediately preceding economic reform and so raise questions on the success of the reform measures. It is thus imperative to probe whether the present situation can be attributed to half-hearted economic reform measures that could not remove the supply constraints, or to the demand

Table 3.1 Growth in India's Foreign Trade

Amount in US $ millions

Period	Export		Import		Balance of trade	Export as % of import
	Amount	% Change	Amount	% Change		
Apr.–Jun. 1991	3990	–	4505	–	-515	89
Jul 1991–Mar 1992	13876	15.9*	14906	10.3*	-1030	93
Apr 1992–Mar 1993	18537	3.8	21882	12.6	-3345	83
Apr 1993–Mar 1994	22238	20.0	23306	6.5	-1068	95
Apr 1994–Mar 1995	26330	18.4	28654	22.9	-2324	92
Apr 1995–Mar 1996	31797	20.8	36678	28.0	-4881	87
Apr 1996–Mar 1997	33470	5.3	39132	6.7	-5663	86
Apr 1997–Mar 1998	35006	4.6	41484	6.0	-6478	84
Apr 1998–Mar 1999	33659	-3.9	41858	0.9	-8199	80

* Growth rate is computed on the basis of monthly average.

Sources: 1. Government of India, (1998) *Economic Survey 1997–8*, New Delhi: Ministry of Finance, p. S-81.
2. Reserve Bank of India, (1997) *Annual Report 1996–7*, Bombay, p.214.
3. Reserve Bank of India, (1999) *Annual Report 1998–9*, Bombay, p. 224.

constraints that lie beyond the control of the Indian Government, or to a combination of both.[1]

Factors Constraining Export Performance

Supply constraints have been related to a shortfall in production, rising cost and inferior quality of exports, and to domestic market being more attractive. Production shortfall is often found in the case of agricultural products due to erratic climatic factors. When production drops, the normal ability to export falls. Moreover, the domestic market prices rise which make the domestic market more lucrative. The incentive to export such goods is badly affected. Sometimes, to assure the domestic supply of such goods, the Government prohibits exports for a certain period as in the case of onions during 1998–9.

The high cost and inferior quality can be attributed to outdated techniques of production. India has been importing technology for decades. During the period of reform, the size of foreign direct investment has risen substantially and, as a result, a growing number of Indian firms are able to make use of improved imported technology. However, the share of foreign investment in total domestic investment is still low compared to that of some other countries that compete with India in the export business (Srinivasan, 1998).

Ghemawat and Patibandla (1999) are of the view that it is the high tariffs, despite cuts in rates during the period of reform, and the distorted excise duty structure, that are responsible for the high cost of Indian exports. Indian exporters of textiles have especially been hurt on this count.

Besides, the risen cost of Indian exports in many cases can also be attributed to poor infrastructural facilities. This relationship between the poor infrastructural facilities and the risen cost of the exports has been examined by Wheeler and

---

[1] The factors constraining export from India during early decades of planning were normally grouped under two heads: supply constraints and demand constraints (Bauer, 1961, Krueger, 1961 and Patel, 1959). In the post-reform period, thus, the constraints are analysed from these two angles.

Mody (1992). For example, it takes five to six days for freighters to turn around in Bombay ports as compared to six to twelve hours in South-east Asian ports. A World Bank study finds the comparative cost disadvantage to Indian exporters as high as $ 80 per container (Srinivasan, 1998).

The infrastructural constraints in India have been reported in other studies too. Dhar and Roy (1999) find that the allocations made in the budget for the development of infrastructural facilities in recent years have been too low to provide sufficient incentives for investors to repose faith in the economy. Kundra (2000) has explained that the lack of infrastructural facilities is one of the major impediments to the growth of export among the Indian export-processing zones. Even the Government admits such constraints (GOI, 1997). However, the recent move to open the infrastructure sector to private initiatives should overcome this bottleneck in future.

Turning to the demand constraints, the basic argument is that a depreciation of currency leads to increased foreign demand and thus greater export earnings. In India, there is a marked depreciation in the value of rupee—a drastic cut in July 1991 and the following depreciation from Rs 31.40/$ in 1994–5 to Rs 33.45/$ in 1995–6 and to Rs 35.50/$ in 1996–7. A big fall in the value of the rupee was witnessed during late 1997 and during 1998 when it crossed Rs 42 a dollar. In 1999 the rupee plunged further to over Rs 43 a dollar (GOI, 1999; RBI, 1999). Surprisingly, this depreciation did not encourage exports. The Research Bureau of Business Standard (BS) carried out a study covering 45 traders and found that the net exchange earnings had gone down in those cases due to the crumbling rupee. The rate of decline in net foreign exchange earnings was very steep in many cases (BS, 17 January 1998). In fact, there is always a time lag between changes in the external value of currency and the resultant changes in the volume of export. During this time lag, which is represented by the first phase of the J-curve effect, depreciation of currency deteriorates the balance of trade further. The Indian case, it can be said, resembles this first phase.

The fall in the external value of the rupee cannot be thought of in isolation of the fall in the value of many East Asian currencies. During the period between July 1997 to January

1999, the rupee dropped by 15.7 per cent, while such a drop in the value of some East Asian currencies had ranged between 30 per cent and 73.4 per cent (GOI, 1999). The countries whose currency has so slumped compete with India in the export of textiles and agricultural products. Since these two groups of commodities account for a sizeable part of India's export, the depreciation of the rupee could not have a favourable impact on exports.

The depreciation in the value of the rupee failed to encourage export because the appreciation in the value of the dollar against some major currencies in the international market and the resultant big cross-currency variations along with the changes in the inflation rate differentials had led to an upsurge in the real effective exchange rate of the rupee.[2] In other words, it was the appreciation in the real effective exchange rate that nullified the favourable effects of the depreciation of the rupee. The Ministry of Finance lists this factor as one of the export constraints (GOI, 1999).

The absence of enhanced demand can also be attributed to some other factors. The financial crisis in East Asian developing countries led to a shrinkage in their demand for Indian goods. Since these countries account for a good part of India's export, the country's export earnings could not move up. Besides, there was also the financial crisis in Russia and Japan that had an adverse impact on the demand for Indian goods in those countries. Moreover, the growth rate of import of some other advanced countries too has turned lower since 1996. These factors have definitely influenced India's export earnings in an adverse way.

This is not all. Some major importers of Indian products have resorted to various kinds of non-tariff barriers (NTBs),

[2] The effective exchange rate may be nominal or real. The nominal effective exchange rate may be defined as a weighted geometric average of the bilateral nominal exchange rates of the home currency in terms of select foreign currencies. The real effective exchange rate takes into account additionally the inflation rate differential. In other words, it may be defined as the weighted average of nominal effective exchange rate adjusted by the ratio of domestic inflation rate to foreign inflation rate. The concept finds place in the study of Hirsch and Higgins (1970) and Rhomberg (1976) and of RBI (1998).

despite the WTO's crusade against the imposition of such barriers. The country's export of textiles, engineering products, chemicals and pharmaceuticals, and agricultural and marine products have been affected on this count. The following sections discuss some more details about this type of demand constraint.

WTO Provisions and the Country's Export

India's external sector reforms coincided with the conclusion of Uruguay Round discussions and the establishment of the WTO. It is a fact that the earlier rounds of GATT did axe tariffs and NTBs in order to promote world trade, but the new regime laid more emphasis on reducing and removing these barriers. It embraced, among other things, provisions for reducing tariffs and securing them against subsequent increases. The provisions went on to eliminate the NTBs over a specific period because it was clear on the issue that protection would be given only through tariffs.

It was hoped that India would gain through these measures but, unfortunately, the major importers of Indian products, viz. the US, EU countries and Japan claiming for around one-half of India's exports, have made use of the safeguard clauses and some other clauses and put severe restrictions on imports from India. Here it may be mentioned that safeguard clauses allow imposition of NTBs in case of injury to domestic industry or in some special cases. But the special cases have become a general case. To cite a few examples, the US Government restricts the import of certain food products, such as uncooked meat products, eggs, fish products, and dairy products on the ground of quarantine and other phyto-sanitary requirements. In 1994, it recalled India-made *ghagras* as they did not meet the flammability standards under the Consumers' Product Safety Act. 'Section 301' restrictions are also there that have affected 40 Indian export organizations and over 200 entities. The Glen Amendment put further restrictions on exports in the wake of the nuclear tests in India in 1998. Anti-dumping and countervailing duties are allowed by the WTO only in exceptional circumstances. But the US Government has been found using them against a number of Indian products.

In the European Union, anti-dumping duty is imposed on Indian steel and textiles. The phyto-sanitary regulations prohibit import of Indian fruit and meat products. Japan, too, applies similar restrictions. There is import ban/quota facing a number of India's agricultural products. Indian *basmati* rice has been a case in point, although it has found a way into the Japanese market, at least to some extent, after much negotiation. A number of similar products have suffered on account of a long wait in Japanese laboratories for obtaining test certificates under phyto-sanitary regulations. Indian export of grapes and banana was doing well till 1993, but strict regulations on their imports into Japan have marred their export.

In recent years, some major importers of Indian goods have implemented the social clause as well as environmental clause. They have restricted the import of Indian carpets because it involves child labour. Similarly, the import of tuna, prawns, and shrimps has been restricted by the US Government on account of the environmental clause. Since the WTO has so far no specific agreement on these issues, these clauses are easily implemented by the importing countries.

There is, of course, the provision for the settlement of disputes if any NTB is unwarranted. Though the dispute was settled in India's favour in the case of shrimp exports, the process of dispute settlement is time consuming. In certain key areas, the rule-oriented dispute settlement system has been constructed in such a way that it leaves open vast imperatives through which the stronger trade partners can safeguard their own interest (Chimni, 1999). Thus the demand constraints do exist despite the best endeavour of the WTO to do away with them.

Greater Penetration into the International Market

It is really important for a country that its export should increase both in absolute and relative terms. It means a greater penetration of the country's exports into the world market. Statistics show that India's share in the world export went up from 0.5 per cent in 1990 and 1992 to 0.6 per cent in 1995 and to 0.7 per cent in 1996. But the extent of penetration is still quite small. The commodity-wise picture shows that out of 47 commodities listed, only 22 commodities have registered an upward move in their relative share. The share of seven commodities stands unchanged, while that of 18 commodities has declined. The commodity-group, where the country's share has increased at the fastest rate, is that of pearls and precious stones. On the contrary, in case of tea and mate, the share has fallen from 22.1 per cent in 1990 to 11.2 per cent in 1995 and from 13.4 per cent to 6.9 per cent in case of leather manufactures (GOI, 1999).

Diversification of Export Market

The saying, 'Do not keep all eggs in the same basket' applies well to the foreign trade sector. If the export market is concentrated, volatility in export earnings will be larger. This is why it is worth examining whether the reform measures have encouraged the diversification of the export market. Table 3.2 shows the share of different countries or the groups of countries importing Indian goods. It is evident that during 1990-1, the year immediately preceding the reform era, the top five countries, viz. the US, Japan, Germany, Russia, and the UK accounted for 54.4 per cent of India's export. By 1997-8, their share dropped to 39.1 per cent in favour of other countries. On the other hand, the share of developing countries — both oil-exporting and net-oil-importing countries — climbed up from 22.4 per cent to 38.2 per cent during this period. All this shows market diversification and also a move towards growing trade with the developing countries. It is a positive signal of reform measures.

We have attempted to estimate market diversification more precisely for which Gini co-efficient of concentration index has been computed. All importing countries have been taken into account, although the members of the Commonwealth of Independent States (CIS) have been treated as one unit. The result shows that the concentration co-efficient has diminished from 0.273905 in 1990-1 to 0.206818 during 1996-7. This diminution, which means greater market diversification, is a positive aspect of foreign trade reform.

Table 3.2   India's Major Export Markets

| | % share in total | |
Market	1990–1	1997–8
US	14.7	19.5
Japan	9.3	5.5
Germany	7.8	5.5
UK	6.5	6.0
OPEC	5.6	10.0
Russia	16.1	2.6
Non-oil developing countries	16.8	28.2

Source: Government of India (1999), *Economic Survey 1998–9*, New Delhi: Ministry of Finance.

Product Diversification

Product diversification is also a healthy sign for the foreign trade sector. This is because product concentration leads to large-scale fluctuation in export earnings. At present in India, over three-fourths of the total export comprise manufactures and slightly less than one-fifth of the total export earnings comes through the export of agricultural and allied products. A very small segment is represented by the export of ores and minerals and crude and petroleum products and a few unclassified items. Table 3.3 shows the export in value terms of four top manufactures and of the agricultural products. In 1990–1, the year immediately preceding initiation of reforms, the share of the top four groups of commodities in the manufactures group was 57.4 per cent of the total export which went down to 47.2 per cent in 1998–9 in favour of other commodities. The share of agricultural commodities too fell marginally in favour of large number of manufactures during this period. This shows a clear-cut trend towards product diversification. For a precise estimate of commodity diversification, Gini-co-efficient of concentration index is found out taking into account two-digit commodities from 01 to 99. The result shows that the concentration index has fallen from 0.232687 in 1991–2 to 0.227510 in 1996–7. This is a positive feature of reform measures.

Table 3.3   Product Pattern of India's Export

Commodity Group	1990-1		1998-9	
	Amount $ mill.	% share	Amount $ mill.	%share
Gems and jewellery	2924	16.1	5904	17.5
Textile fabrics and manufactures	3807	21.0	3943	11.7
Garment	2236	12.3	4444	13.2
Leather manufactures	1449	8.0	1620	4.8
Total manufactures	13229	72.9	25797	76.6
Agricultural products	3521	19.4	5996	17.8
Total (including others)	18143	100.0	33659	100.0

Sources: 1.Government of India (1999), *Economic Survey 1998-9* New Delhi: Ministry of Finance.
2. Reserve Bank of India (1999), *Annual Report 1998-9* Bombay.

Terms of Trade

The success of reform measures also depends upon whether the terms of trade have moved in India's favour. Fortunately, the figures confirm this view. Table 3.4 presents the figures of gross barter, net barter and income terms of trade. Gross barter terms of trade imply volume index of exports expressed as a percentage of volume index of imports. Net barter terms of trade imply unit value index of exports expressed as percentage of unit value index of imports. Income terms of trade imply the product of net barter terms of trade and volume index of export expressed as percentage.

It is found that gross barter terms of trade index (Base year = 1978-9) fell slightly in the first year of reform, but then they began improving till 1994-5 when the index touched 139.5. However, they receded during the following two fiscal years reaching 124.3 in 1996-7. Almost similar was the case with the net barter terms of trade. The index improved from 119.5 in 1991-92 to 152.4 in 1994-5 but then it dropped gradually to 126.2 in 1996-7. The income terms of trade improved substantially during the period of reform – from 249.3 in 1991-2 to 530 in 1995-6, although dipping marginally to 519.7 in

1996–7. All this means large gains from trade accruing to India during the post-reform period.

Table 3.4   India's Terms of Trade
(Base Year = 1978–9)

Year	Gross barter	Net barter	Income
1990–1	122.5	109.3	212.2
1991–2	109.3	119.5	249.3
1992–3	126.5	127.3	283.8
1993–4	127.8	144.9	373.1
1994–5	139.5	152.4	446.0
1995–6	134.0	137.9	530.0
1996–7	124.3	126.2	519.7

Source: Government of India (1998), *Economic Survey 1997–8* New Delhi: Ministry of Finance.

Stability in Export Earnings

Last but not least, reform in foreign trade sector can be said to be positive if India's export earnings get stabilized. It is because instability in export earnings retards the ability to import and hampers the process of economic development. To examine the impact of reform process on stability of export earnings, we have taken into account the export figures during 1984–91 (pre-reform period) and those during 1992–9, the period of economic reform. The instability index is computed for these two periods and then the two indices are compared. It may be mentioned that for calculating the index, we have adopted the method suggested by Massell (1970) where the index is represented by the standard deviation of the residual from the trend and the trend is estimated by the ordinary least squares.

The computation of the indices shows that the instability index moved up from 1164.1709 during the pre-reform period to 2230.1002 during the period of reform. In other words, reform in foreign trade sector has failed to promote stability in export earning which is actually desired for strengthening the process of economic development. This negates the efficacy of reform measures.

Conclusion

In short, foreign trade sector reforms have not lived up to expectations. It is true that the terms of trade have gone in India's favour conferring upon it gains from trade. It is also true that the structure of trade has diversified in favour of larger number of commodities and countries that is a positive trend. However, the trade deficit has been on the increase despite lowering of the growth rate of imports in recent years making the development process more vulnerable. There are, of course, some supply constraints that the Indian government has not been able to remove completely. But more importantly, there are external factors not within the control of the Indian Government that have been responsible for slow growth of exports. The budget proposals for 1999–2000 include the creation of a gold deposit scheme, as a result of which hoarded gold is expected to come out that will lower the gold import bill. The budget proposals also aim at providing export credits at internationally prevailing interest rates and at reducing procedural bottlenecks. Good results are expected if the supply constraints are removed and the world economy makes favourable growth.

4

Foreign Direct Investment

The economic reform measures might not have substantially bridged the current account deficit, but they have definitely encouraged the process of foreign direct investment (FDI) into the country. This is why, whenever one talks about economic reform in India's external sector, discussions on FDI have great importance. The present chapter probes deep into the various aspects of FDI flowing into this country.

Measures of FDI Policy Reform

Broadly speaking, the new policy helps increase the stake of foreign investors in Indian companies, provides a bigger room for their entry, axes the procedural formalities, provides additive incentives for the import of technology and to the NRIs and in all creates a congenial environment for FDI.

Diluting the provisions of the FERA, the new policy removes the 40 per cent ceiling for foreign equity participation that existed during the pre-reform period. Moreover, it provides for automatic approval of foreign collaborations in many cases. In case of nine categories of industries, viz. mining services, basic metal and alloys, electric generation and transmission, non-conventional energy generation and distribution, construction, land and water transport, storage and warehousing services and some manufactures like industrial and scientific instruments, the RBI grants automatic approval of foreign collaborations even if foreign participation in equity goes up to 74 per cent. In case of infrastructural projects of this group, automatic approval can be availed even with 100 per cent foreign equity participation. In 48 categories of industries, automatic approval is granted if the foreign equity participation goes up to 51 per cent. In case of three categories of industries, such as mining of iron ore, metal ore and non-metallic minerals, foreign equity participation should not exceed 50 per cent if automatic approval is expected. The Budget proposals for 1999–2000 aim at widening the list of automatic approvals covering important industrial and services sectors (GOI, 1999a).

If a foreign investor wishes to have greater participation in equity than that mentioned above, documents have to be routed through the Foreign Investment Promotion Board (FIPB) which is under the Industry Ministry of the Indian Government. The FIPB sanctions even 100 per cent equity participation in cases where Indian companies are unable to raise funds or in cases where at least one-half of output is meant for export. It is done also in cases where foreign investor is to bring in proprietary technology (IIC, 1997a).

The new policy extends FDI to trading, hotels and tourism-related companies, units of export-processing zones and 100 per cent EOUs, banking and non-banking financial services, of course, with varying degree of foreign equity participation. The non-banking financial services now include credit-card and money-changing businesses. The multilateral financial institutions are allowed to contribute equity to the extent of shortfall in the holdings of NRIs within the overall permissible limit of 40 per cent in the public sector banks. FDI is also allowed in those areas where the big industrial houses were not previously allowed to invest. The new policy permits opening of branch/liaison offices of foreign companies, revoking the prohibition of 1973. The branch office can be set up for conducting research and development, undertaking export/import activities and for making available desired technology. An off-shore venture capital company may contribute to an entire equity base of a domestic venture capital fund and may also set up a domestic asset management company (IIC, 1997a).

FDI does not always involve investment in cash. A purely technical collaboration involves permission to use patents or trademark and transfer of technology for which the Indian company pays royalty, technical service fees, etc. In case of technology import, too, the new policy provides for automatic approval if the collaboration agreement involves royalty payment up to $ 2 million (net of taxes) to be made in a lump-sum amount or up to 5 per cent of domestic sale and 8 per cent of export over a ten-year period from the date of agreement or seven years from the date of commencement of business. As regards hiring of foreign technicians, there is no bar if the RBI guidelines are followed. There is no bar also on the use of foreign brand name.

The policy cuts the procedural delays significantly. Automaticity of approvals is a case in point. Abolition of industrial licensing almost in all cases (except public sector units and those units producing hazardous items) is another example. The Foreign Investment Promotion Council was set up in 1996 to identify projects within the country that require foreign investment and to target specific countries from where FDI can be brought in (IIC, 1997a). To foster speedy approvals, the FIPB has been asked to give its decision within a period of 30 days. For speedy implementation of the approved investment, the government has set up the Foreign Investment Implementation Authority that convened its first meeting in the last week of September 1999.

NRIs making FDI get special treatment. They make direct investments either on repatriable terms or on non-repatriable terms. In case of repatriable investments, their share can go up to 100 per cent of the equity if the project concerns high-priority industry, housing and real-estate development, air-taxi operations, sick unit, 100 per cent export-oriented units or a unit in export-processing zone and a trading house. On non-repatriable terms, NRIs' participation can go up to 100 per cent of bonus issues in an Indian company if the company is not engaged in agriculture, real estate, or plantation. Non-repatriable investment can also flow into proprietary/ partnership concerns engaged in industrial, trading and commercial activities (IIC, 1997b). Further details are elaborated in the next chapter.

The Indian government is quite liberal regarding dividend repatriation abroad. There is no bar if taxes are paid. However, in a limited number of consumer goods, such outflow has to be balanced with export earnings for a period of seven years. Disinvestment too can be made subject to a few RBI formalities.

In all, the Indian government has created a healthy atmosphere for FDI inflow. It is now a member of the Multilateral Investment Guarantee Agency (MIGA) which has infused confidence among foreign investors against expropriation of assets. What is important is that despite change in government in the country, economic reform process has never been neglected. The present Government is also moving in the same direction. The Finance Minister has welcomed foreign investment in sectors of national interest, such as infrastructure, core industries, and export-promoting sector as well as in the case of some consumer-good industries if it requires improved technology (Business Standard, 6 April 1998).

Impact of the Reforms

A probe into the impact of the new policy involves *inter alia* a few questions regarding:

- the size of FDI and if it has increased
- the number of investors and countries interested in investing in India
- FDI movement into bigger areas of the economy
- the share of foreign investors in the equity of the Indian companies

The answers to these questions will show whether the impact of the new policy has been positive.

Size of FDI

The impact of the new policy on the magnitude of the FDI inflow can be analysed from two angles: one from the angle of approvals and the other from the angle of actual inflow.

Table 4.1 shows that the amount of approved investment during the period of reform has been much larger than in the pre-reform period. As compared to approved investment for Rs 12.7 billion during the whole of the decade beginning from 1981 (GOI, 1992), the figure of approved investment during August-December 1991 stood at Rs 4.128 billion. It was Rs 38.875 billion during 1992 that shot up to Rs 88.593 billion in 1993, Rs 141.872 billion in 1994, Rs 320.717 billion in 1995 and to Rs 361.468 billion in 1996. It was as high as Rs 548.914 billion in 1997. In fact, the foreign investors rated India as the country of their choice in the wake of liberalization. The amount of approved investment slumped to Rs 308.135 billion during 1998. This slump can be attributed to a host of factors, important among them being the political instability in the country, poor domestic industrial environment and the unfavourable external economic factors, such as financial crisis in south-east Asia, etc. However, the scenario tended to improve during the first half of 1999 as the monthly average of approved investment began to get larger. During the whole of the first six months of 1999, FDI for Rs 162.400 billion was approved. This was perhaps the result of the renewed faith of the foreign investors in the Indian economy.

In the period of reform, the number of collaboration agreements increased but not at a galloping speed. Table 4.1 shows that financial collaborations have gradually outnumbered the purely technical collaborations. This is because of relaxation in investment norms.

As far as the quantum of actual inflow of FDI is concerned, the picture is not so bright as that of the approved investment amount. In 1991, the amount of approved investment was small and so it was easy for actual inflow to account for 64 per cent of the approved amount. But with fast growth in approvals, the actual inflow failed to keep pace with the approved investment. The percentage lagged far behind. The ratio of actual inflow to approved amount was as low as 17.8 per cent during 1992. However, it improved to over one-fifth in the following years till 1997 and was as large as 43.23 per cent in 1998 and 47.59 per cent in the first half of 1999. The upward movement in the ratio of actual flow in recent years is a redeeming feature.

Table 4.1 Size of FDI

Amount in Rs billions

Period	No. of collaborations		Approved foreign investment	Actual inflow amount	Actual inflow as % of approved	Exchange rate: Rs/$
	Technical	Financial				
Aug–Dec 1991	491	175	4.128	2.656*	64.34	24.47
1992	839	691	38.875	6.912	17.78	26.43
1993	691	785	88.593	18.620	21.02	31.37
1994	792	1090	141.872	31.122	21.94	31.40
1995	882	1355	320.717	64.853	20.22	33.45
1996	774	1559	361.468	84.484	23.37	35.50
1997	660	1665	548.914	120.357	21.93	37.17
1998	595	1191	308.135	133.204	43.23	42.38
Jan–Jun 1999	215	752	162.400	77.287	47.59	43.38

*The figure relates to the whole of the year.
Note: The exchange rate is the annual average. It relates to financial years between 1991 and 1997. For 1998, it is that prevailing in December 1998. For January to June 1999, it relates to that on the 30th June.
Source: Foreign Investment Promotion Board documents.

In fact, approval does not imply that the follow-up action is immediate. Many formalities are required after a collaboration agreement is approved. In case of automatic approval, the procedural formalities are not so cumbersome as in the case of approvals through the FIPB route. However, they exist. In case of approvals through the FIPB route, the files move through different ministries and departments that often work at cross purposes with each other (Joshi and D'souza, 1999). Red-tapism exists at every step. This is perhaps the reason that the ratio of actual inflow to the approved amount is much lower in case of the approvals through FIPB. And since the FIPB approvals account for a lion's share of the total approved amount, the ratio of actual inflow on the whole is very low (Gupta, 1998). However, with the establishment of the Foreign Investment Implementation Authority, this problem should not matter much as this authority will bring in smooth co-ordination between different ministries and departments.

Again, lack of sufficient infrastructural facilities sometimes comes in the way of implementation of a project. In absence of sufficient infrastructural support, the implementation of a project may be delayed considerably or, in some cases, it may even be denied. This has actually happened in case of the projects under foreign collaboration. Brahmbhatta et al. (1996) have found this very factor a significant one in the Indian case and so they have argued for the creation of adequate infrastructural facilities for encouraging greater flow of FDI. Yet again, in a federal structure of administration, the state governments have to co-operate with the coming up of the project. But in many cases, it is found that the required response from the state governments has been absent (Bhattacharya, 1994).

FDI Flow in a Comparative Perspective

It is evident from the preceding discussion of the present section that the size of approved FDI or the quantum of actual FDI inflow or the ratio of actual flow to the approved investment has gone up during the period of reform. Nevertheless, it is worth analysing whether the FDI inflow in

India can be compared with that in some other countries of Asia where openness or liberal economic policies exist. Statistics show that the annual average of the FDI flow into India during 1992–7 was $ 1.6 billion compared to $ 29.8 billion in China, $ 6.6 billion in Singapore, $ 3.6 billion in Indonesia, $ 4.5 billion in Malaysia and $ 2.2 billion in Thailand during the same period, despite the fact that India accounted for around three-fourths of the FDI flow into South Asian countries (United Nations, 1998). All this means that the economic reforms in India have still a long way to go to attract FDI flow into the country.

Sources of FDI

One has to analyse whether the new policy has been able to broaden the source of FDI into India. There were 86 countries in 1998 as compared to 29 countries in 1991 whose FDI was approved by the Indian Government. Thus, the number of countries investing in India has increased during the period of reform. But still a lion's share of FDI comes from only a few countries. Table 4.2 shows the investment of top seven countries that was approved during the period January 1991 to December 1998. The US alone accounted for a quarter of the approved investment, followed by Mauritius which shared another one-tenth of it. The other five countries, viz. the UK, Japan, Germany, South Korea, and Australia collectively shared 21.67 per cent of approved investment. This means that only seven countries accounted for well over 56 per cent of the investment approved during the above period. Nevertheless, the geographic concentration in the reform period is lower than that in the pre-reform period. In 1990, only six countries, viz. the US, the UK, Germany, Japan, Italy, and France were responsible for over two-thirds of the approved investment (IIC, 1991).

This is not all. During the liberal regime beginning from August 1991, developing countries, such as Mauritius, South Korea, Malaysia, Cayman Islands and many others have made their appearance on the list of major investors (SIA Newsletter, October 1998). The developing countries investing sizeably in India can be grouped broadly into two sets. The first set is

Table 4.2   Major County-wise FDI Approvals in India
(Jan 1991–Dec 1998)

Country	Approved investment Rs billion	% Share in total approved investment	Actual inflow Rs billion	Actual inflow as % of approved investment
US	426.093	24.16	65.430	15.56
Mauritius	183.953	10.37	105.753	57.49
UK	130.136	6.89	18.319	14.08
Japan	75.130	4.27	23.337	31.06
Germany	67.603	3.79	21.529	31.85
South Korea	60.412	3.46	19.263	31.89
Australia	59.063	3.26	1.693	2.87

Source: Foreign Investment Promotion Board documents.

represented by those developing countries that have developed their industrial base with the help of technology imported from the industrialized world and are now in a position to provide technology and capital to the Indian enterprises. Singapore, South Korea, and Malaysia are some examples. On the other hand, the second set of developing countries are those that have not so far developed their industrial base to that extent. Rather they are tax-haven countries, such as Mauritius and Cayman Islands. Since the tax rates in these countries are very low, the multinational corporations headquartered in other countries—developed as well as developing—are found diverting their receipt of funds on different accounts to these tax havens. In other words, these countries play hosts for cash positioning of the multinational companies. This way they possess huge investible surplus, a part of which has found its way into India. As mentioned earlier, Mauritius alone accounts for around one-tenth of FDI approved by the Indian Government during the period of economic reforms. A lion's share of such investment is represented by the holding companies of Mauritius set up by the US firms. It means that the investment flowing from the tax havens is mainly the investment of the multinational corporations headquartered in other countries. Now an important question arises as to why the US companies have routed their investment through Mauritius. It is because, firstly, the US companies have positioned their funds in Mauritius which they like to invest somewhere. Secondly, because the tax treaty between Mauritius and India stipulates a dividend tax of five per cent, while the treaty between India and the US stipulates a dividend tax of 15 per cent (United Nations, 1999). However, the present move among the tax havens to align their tax structure in conformity with those in the OECD countries is expected to discourage channelling of FDI through them in future.

When ones looks at the sources of FDI from the viewpoint of actual inflow, it is not Australia, rather the Netherlands, that figures among the top seven countries (see Table 4.2). These countries account for 82.65 per cent of the actual inflow of FDI during 1991–8 that shows a very high degree of geographic concentration, much higher than found from the figures of approved investment. However, the ratio of actual inflow to approved investment varies widely from one case to another. It is evident from Table 4.2 that it was as high as 57.49 per cent in case of Mauritius and as low as 2.87 per cent in case of Australia. One fact evident from this type of wide variation is that the investing firms and not merely the factors operating in the host country, are responsible for a low ratio of actual inflow to approved investment.

Sectoral Pattern

Whether the opening up of many areas of the economy for FDI has any impact on the sectoral pattern of investment is a question of some importance. For the pre-reform period, that is for 1990, the figures for sector-wise approved collaborations are available. They show that six industries/sectors, viz. electrical equipment, telecommunication, industrial machinery, miscellaneous mechanical and engineering industries, chemicals (other than fertilizers) and consultancy services shared collectively 68.1 per cent of the total number of collaborations (IIC, 1991). But during the period of reform covering August 1991 through December 1998, the share of the above six industries, as shown in Table 4.3, came down to 45.6 per cent of total number of collaborations. On the other hand, food-processing industry, which had shared barely 1 per cent of the collaborations in 1990, attracted around 4.91 per cent of them during the reform period. Hotels and tourism, services and trading companies that were absent from the list in 1990, accounted for about 8.92 per cent of the collaborations from August 1991 to December 1998. Collaborations totalling 526 were agreed upon in the area of fuel and power and 703 agreements were concluded in automobile industry.

The figures in Table 4.3 reveal that the number of technical collaborations was larger than that of financial collaborations in metallurgical industry, industrial machinery, chemicals, drugs and pharmaceutical industry and a few others in view of the fact that they required primarily improved technology. In other cases, it was availability of foreign exchange that was more important and so the number of financial collaborations was larger.

Table 4.3 also shows the sector-wise investment approved during the period of reform ranging from August 1991 to December 1998. Fuel and power reigned supreme claiming Rs 577.797 billion or 31.87 per cent of the total approved investment. More than one-half of this amount was approved during 1997. The next in order was telecommunication sector that accounted for Rs 327.409 billion or 18.06 per cent of total approved investment. This means that these two sectors alone were responsible for almost half of the approved investment. Among the major traditional recipients of FDI were the metallurgical industry, electrical equipment, and chemicals (other than fertilizers) that collectively claimed 17.59 per cent. In the transportation industry, which shared 6.18 per cent of the approved amount, the automobile sector alone accounted for over two-thirds of the amount. A few other consumer goods industries, such as textiles, food-processing and fermentation industry, paper, pulp and paper products, and glass industry collectively accounted for 8.78 per cent of the approved amount. Food-processing industry was the largest recipient in this sector in view of the agrarian base of the economy. Consultancy services shared not even one per cent of the amount in view of strengthening of the domestic

Table 4.3   Sectoral Pattern of FDI Approvals
(Aug 1991 to Dec 1998)

Industry/sector	No. of collaborations			Approved FDI	
	Total	Tech.	Financial	Rs billion	% of Total
1. Metallurgical industry	539	295	244	111.497	6.15
2. Fuel and power	526	162	364	577.797	31.87
3. Electrical equipment	2490	987	1503	91.156	5.25
4. Telecommunication	478	109	369	327.409	18.06
5. Transportation industry	895	433	462	112.067	6.18
of which: automobiles	703	396	307	78.345	
6. Industrial machinery	1161	736	425	19.584	1.08
7. Chemicals	1364	698	666	112.302	6.19
(other than fertilizers)					
8. Textiles	547	114	433	28.069	1.55
9. Food-processing	698	137	561	83.406	4.60
10. Fermentation	58	17	41	11.255	0.62
11. Drugs & pharmaceuticals	307	171	136	8.020	0.44
12. Paper, pulp & paper products	152	62	90	23.087	1.27
13. Glass	78	28	50	13.417	0.74
14. Consultancy services	424	80	344	17.082	0.94
15. Services	590	36	554	115.696	6.38
of which: financial	241	6	235	71.440	

Table 4.3 contd.

Table 4.3 contd.

Industry/sector	No. of collaborations			Approved FDI	
	Total	Tech.	Financial	Rs billion	% of Total
16. Hotels and tourism	328	112	216	34.906	1.93
of which: hotels, restaurants	262	93	169	27.637	
17. Trading	351	16	335	12.188	0.67
Total incl. others	14230	5718	8512	1812.966	100.00

Source: Foreign Investment Promotion Board Documents.

consultancy base. But the services, especially the financial ones received Rs 115.696 billion or 6.38 per cent of the approved investment. The share of hotels and tourism was 1.93 per cent but that of trading companies was less than one per cent.

The sectoral pattern of FDI based on the actual inflow is clear from Table 4.4. The figures show that there are seven sectors that have attracted 43.32 per cent of the total inflow during 1991–8. They are not simply the traditional sectors, such as electrical equipment, telecommunication, transportation industry, and chemical industry (other than fertilizers), but also the non-traditional recipients of FDI, such as food-processing industry, service sector and fuels. These three non-traditional sectors alone received around one-sixth of the FDI flow during 1991-1998.

Table 4.4   Sectoral Pattern of Actual FDI Inflow
(1991–8)

Sector	Actual inflow Rs billion	% of total	Actual inflow as % of approved investment
Transportation industry	47.719	7.97	42.58
Electrical equipment	43.277	7.23	47.48
Telecommunications	38.642	6.46	11.80
Chemicals (other than fertilisers)	38.551	6.44	34.33
Services	40.122	6.71	34.67
Fuels	30.796	5.15	55.21
Food-processing industries	20.105	3.36	24.10
Total	598.364	100.00	

Note: The percentage in the third column has been computed without excluding the unclassified figures of investment inflow.
Source: Foreign Investment Promotion Board documents.

However, the ratio of actual inflow to the approved investment has varied widely among the sectors. It is as high as 55.21 per cent in case of fuels and as low as 11.80 per cent in case of telecommunications. This type of diversity shows that it is also the nature of the sectors that has influence on the approval-inflow lag.

Extent of Foreign Participation in Equity

Removal of the ceiling on foreign equity participation must have an impact on the equity pattern of the Indian companies that have gone for foreign collaboration. In fact, foreign investors prefer to have dominating role in the management of the company so that their interest behind inter-nationalization is served without resistance. If rules and regulations in the host country are not very rigid on the issue of foreign equity participation, it is natural for them to go for majority shareholding. This has actually happened in India in the wake of relaxation of regulations on this count during the period of reform. Table 4.5 shows the extent of foreign equity participation during the period of reform. Figures are available for the period between August 1991 to February 1998 which involved 7535 cases of financial collaborations involving an approved FDI for Rs 1578.903 billion. It is evident from the figures that 100 per cent foreign equity companies constituting 14.8 per cent of the total number of foreign-collaborated companies in India accounted for 31.3 per cent of total approved FDI during the above period. In 7.5 per cent of the foreign-collaborated companies representing foreign equity participation above 74 per cent but below 100 per cent, around 7.0 per cent of the approved FDI was involved. In 8.9 per cent of the cases representing foreign equity participation above 51 per cent and up to 74 per cent 13.7 per cent of the approved FDI was involved. In the rest 68.8 per cent cases representing foreign equity participation up to 51 per cent, less than half of the approved FDI was involved. From available consolidated figures, foreign equity participation ranged from 74 percent to 100 per cent in 500 cases out of 932 cases of financial collaborations approved during the first nine months of 1998 (FIPB documents). All this shows that larger FDI is marked in cases representing greater shareholding by foreign investors.

Table 4.5   Equity-range-wise Distribution of FDI Cases
(Aug 1991 to Feb 1998)

Equity range %	Number	Foreign equity Rs billion
< 51	5192	758.298
> 51 and < 74	671	214.232
> 74 and < 100	562	111.923
100	1110	494.449
Total	7535	1578.902

Source: Foreign Investment Promotion Board documents.

Conclusion

The liberal policy towards FDI designed in the wake of structural adjustment and macroeconomic reforms in India since mid-1991 has helped attract foreign investors significantly. The amount of approved investment has grown enormously. Though the actual inflow of FDI has not picked up so fast, it has improved and significantly strengthened the capital account of the balance of payments of the country. Nevertheless, India is still on a lower ladder among some major FDI receiving countries of Asia.

The new policy has attracted investors from different corners of the globe—developed and developing. Nevertheless, well over one-half of the approved amount is claimed by only six or seven countries. Moreover, it is evident that the foreign investors are interested more in investment than in merely supplying technology. This is why the financial collaborations have outnumbered the purely technical collaborations.

The sectoral pattern has come to be greatly broad-based. The traditional recipients have figured large in the approvals as well as in terms of actual inflow of FDI. Yet with the opening up of new areas for foreign investors, a huge amount of approval and actual inflow is also found in non-traditional areas, such as fuel and power, services and some consumer-goods.

The removal of the ceiling from foreign equity participation has manifested in a large number of wholly-owned subsidiaries of foreign companies and in the approval of majority foreign participation in the equity of Indian companies. All this has resulted in the domination of foreign investors.

5

Attracting NRI Investment

The Indian Government relies greatly on the NRIs for greater inflow of foreign investment into this country. It is nothing unexpected, rather it is based on the positive experiences during the 1980s in this country and similar experiences of some other countries like Hungary, Poland, Yugoslavia, and China.

NRIs are very large in number. It is estimated that over fourteen million persons of Indian origin are living in different parts of the world. They have an estimated saving potential of approximately US $ one billion a year (Sharan, 1993). Apart from their saving potential they have acquired, in many cases, superb technical, managerial, and business capabilities that may prove crucial for Indian economic development. In most cases, it could well be their familiarity with the business environment in their mother country that they show interest in the development of the Indian economy. If they find the investment climate in this country favourable, NRIs are likely to transmit foreign exchange, technology and other skills into their mother country.

It was primarily this reason that led the Indian Government to think seriously about this alternative source of foreign exchange during the early 1970s when it introduced two bank deposit schemes, known as the non-resident external rupee account and foreign currency non-resident account. In 1979, a committee was set up under the chairmanship of R. N. Malhotra to examine such foreign-exchange remittances into the country. It was followed by the appointment of a group of experts by the Economic and Administrative Reforms Commission in 1981 for framing a broad NRIs' investment policy. In 1982–3, yet another committee was set up under the chairmanship of Bimal Jalan to suggest how to make maximum use of NRIs' potential. A number of suggestions poured in that were implemented subsequently. In all, a liberal and attractive policy environment was created which led to a massive flow of NRIs' resources into this country from the mid-1980s.

Naturally, when the external sector reforms were launched in 1991, the Indian Government decided to create a more congenial environment for NRIs' investment. It provided them a number of fresh incentives to attract such investment. Now the question is whether the fresh incentives have yielded rich dividends and a greater inflow of funds have really been registered on their account. The purpose of the present chapter is to find an answer to this question.

Modes of NRI Investment

Who are the NRIs and what are the modes of their investment? An NRI is an Indian citizen staying abroad for employment or for carrying out business or vocation. The term also includes a foreign citizen of Indian origin who, at any time, has held an Indian passport or whose parents or grandparents were citizens of India. It also includes overseas corporate bodies (OCBs) predominantly owned by an NRI. Again, the term, 'investment' is used in this chapter in the most generic sense embracing not only direct and portfolio investment but also deposits with Indian banks and non-banking companies and investment in government securities and mutual funds. Each mode has various schemes. Some of the schemes date back to the pre-reform era while some others were added to the list during the reform period. A few others were withdrawn subsequently. This section discusses these schemes briefly to provide a background for the analysis of the impact of the liberal policy during the period of reform.

Regarding bank deposits, NRIs can open accounts both in foreign currency and in rupees. The oldest of the foreign-currency accounts, known as the Foreign Currency Non-resident (FCNR) account was started as far back as in 1975 but was abolished in August 1994. In November 1990, the Foreign Currency Non-resident Non-repatriable Ordinary (FCNRO) account was introduced, but this scheme, too, was withdrawn in August 1994. Presently, the FCNR(B) (Bank Account) is in vogue. It is different from other foreign currency accounts insofar as in this case, the RBI does not provide exchange-rate guarantee to banks for deposits. The foreign-currency account is maintained only in a few designated currencies, such as pound sterling, US dollars, Deutschmark, and Japanese yen. It is maintained only in the form of term deposit for a period ranging from six months to three years after which the deposit is renewed. Repatriation out of such deposits is freely permitted. The interest rate is fixed by the RBI based on the rates prevailing in the international capital market for the respective currency.

The rupee account takes two forms: the Non-resident External Rupee (NRER) account and the Non-resident Non-repatriable Rupee (NRNRR) account. The foreign-currency funds brought in by NRIs are converted at market rates into rupee and then deposited in these accounts. NRER is the oldest account beginning as back as in the early 1970s. The other was introduced during the reform period. NRER account can be maintained in current/saving/fixed deposit form, but NRNRR account is maintained only in the form of fixed deposit. Foreign currency travellers' cheques/notes are freely credited to NRER account. Local funds are also credited if they are of repatriable nature. Local payments are debited freely from NRER account. Nomination is also allowed. The balances held in NRER account can be repatriated abroad. NRNRR account is different from the above as the principal amount along with the interest accrued before October 1994 is non-repatriable. The banks are free to determine the interest rates under this scheme (RBI, 1996).

As regards deposits with public-limited companies, the scheme existed well during the pre-reform period. It still continues in repatriable and non-repatriable forms. Repatriable deposits are meant for a minimum period of three years. Besides these medium-term deposits, the RBI has now

permitted Indian companies to issue commercial papers to
NRIs. Such investments are neither repatriable outside India
nor are they transferable.

NRIs can also invest in government securities. The amount
of such investment can be repatriated abroad if it is made out
of foreign currency. Otherwise, the investment amount after
maturity is credited to the non-resident rupee account. NRIs
can invest in the units of the Unit Trust of India (UTI) and in
national saving certificates (NSC). The terms of repatriation
are the same as in case of investment in government securities.

NRIs can make portfolio investment in India or, in other
words, can acquire shares and debentures of Indian
companies or units of domestic mutual funds through stock
exchanges in India. Their application has to be routed through
designated bank branches that have got the authority from
RBI. The Budget proposals for 1999–2000 aim at simplifying
the mechanism for their investment in mutual funds to a post-
facto reporting mechanism. The ceiling of 1 per cent of the
paid-up share capital of a company in case of an individual
NRI and the overall ceiling of 5 per cent so far applicable to
them were raised to 5 per cent and 10 per cent respectively
under the Budget proposals for 1998–9. This ceiling is
exclusive of the investment ceiling available to the foreign
institutional investors. NRIs can also invest in unlisted
companies. Moreover, the Budget proposals for 1998–9
planned to attract their investment in the UTI and SBI bonds.
Subsequently, Resurgent India Bonds (RIB) were issued by the
State Bank of India or SBI in August 1998. This was in
consonance with Rangarajan Committee recommendations
that had emphasized on attracting medium-term investment
by NRIs.

The most important segment of NRI investment in India is
the direct investment they have been making both on
repatriable and non-repatriable terms since the pre-reform
period. After launching of reform measures, a host of
incentives are being provided to them. Their stake in Indian
companies has been raised. A number of areas have been
made open for their investment. Procedural formalities have
been eased. All these are in line with the incentives provided

to the foreign investors in general. But the NRIs get a few more facilities and are put on to a privileged position. They can now make direct investment on non-repatriable terms in shares/convertible debentures and can make capital contribution to proprietary/partnership concerns on non-repatriable basis if investment does not concern agricultural/ plantation/real-estate activities.

On repatriable terms, NRIs can purchase shares or convertible debentures of Indian companies under 24 per cent scheme, 40 per cent scheme, and 100 per cent scheme. There was the 74 per cent scheme earlier, but with the coming up of 100 per cent scheme, it has lost its significance. Under the 24 per cent scheme, NRIs can invest in the shares or convertible debentures up to 24 per cent of the new issue of Indian companies engaged in financing, hire purchase, leasing, trading, and other services. Under the 40 per cent scheme, the Indian companies can obtain NRIs' direct investment up to 40 per cent of the new issue if they are engaged in industrial and manufacturing activities, hotels, hospitals, and diagnostic centres, shipping, computer software, and oil-exploration services. NRIs can have 100 per cent equity participation in the new issue of a company if it is concerned with high-priority industries, real-estate development, including buildings, township, urban infrastructure, etc, air-taxi operation, trading and export-house activities, and if the company is a unit in an export-processing zone or is a 100 per cent export-oriented unit. NRIs can go for the revival of sick industrial units by making bulk investment up to 100 per cent of the equity. The original investment in this case is repatriable after specified lock-in period (IIC, 1997). The Budget proposals for 1999–2000 extend to the NRIs the facility of automatic approval in all cases of direct investment except for those involving notified FDI equity caps or compulsory licensing or public-sector and small-scale sector reservation (GOI, 1999a).

Besides investment and deposit, NRIs can buy immovable property in India. Those returning to India for permanent settlement can maintain a bank account in foreign currency. These measures attract foreign investment into the country.

Impact of the Reforms

It has been found that the liberal policy of the Indian Government towards NRIs during the 1980s had helped them to make greater investment in this country (Sharan, 1993). Thus it is natural to expect that far greater liberalization in the policy towards NRIs during the reform period should help enhance their investment tremendously into the country. In fact, this is the hypothesis that the present chapter will examine. It may, however, be noted here that unavailability of detailed statistics poses a serious problem. Discrepancy in figures obtained from different governmental agencies poses another serious problem. Nevertheless, limited data available with us will definitely help us to reach a conclusion.

Direct Investment

Table 5.1 shows the magnitude of direct investment approvals under different schemes during the period of reform. For the sake of comparison, the annual average of approved investment during the pre-reform period is also given. The pre-reform period covers from 1984–5 to 1990–1 when the Bimal Jalan Committee recommendations were implemented to attract investment from NRIs. The figures show that the annual average of direct investment approval during 1984–91, which was of the order of Rs 2.5 billion, soared up to over Rs 3.2 billion during 1991–2, Rs 18.5 billion during 1992–3, Rs 25.2 billion in 1993–4 and to Rs 59.8 billion in 1994–5. The amount slipped slightly to Rs 54.4 billion in 1995–6 but again climbed up to Rs 65.9 billion in 1996–7. Again, there was a sharp drop in the approved amount to Rs 28.5 billion during 1997–8 and to Rs 4.2 billion during the first six months of 1998–9 for which data could be available.

It is not easy to hold any particular factor responsible for this downfall during 1997–8 and the first six months of 1998–9, but the slump can be attributed to a host of factors, such as slowing down of the performance of the economy, instability in political atmosphere, and fluctuation in the external value of rupee. Foreign investors are fair-weather friends who invest only when they find the atmosphere congenial.

It is evident from the figures that non-repatriable investment has always been lower than repatriable investment. It is because an investor likes to have the option of repatriation of investment if the latter fails to assure desired returns. Nevertheless, the ratio of non-repatriable segment in the total direct investment was larger during the pre-reform period than in the period of reform. The reason is perhaps the lack of rigidity of exchange-control mechanism governing repatriation during the period of reform that went in favour of repatriable investment. Table 5.1 shows the approval of non-repatriable investment only during two fiscal years, viz. 1991–2 and 1992–3. The following years did witness the actual flow of non-repatriable investment that had been approved till 1992–3. The ratio of non-repatriable investment approval to total direct investment approval was 0.26 per cent during 1991–3 as compared to 16 per cent during 1984–91.

Normally, a foreign investor prefers to invest in cases where it is given a higher share in the equity. But as the figures show, this concept does not necessarily hold good in case of NRIs. During the period of seven-and-a-half years ending June 1998, the approval in case of 40 per cent scheme stood at Rs 130.338 billion compared to Rs 47.842 billion approved under 100 per cent scheme. In case of 100 per cent scheme, largest segment of approval was accounted for by high-priority industries. Real-estate development attracted Rs 35.852 billion. However, the air-taxi scheme attracted barely Rs 1.4 billion. The 24 per cent scheme is of recent origin, yet the approval in this scheme touched Rs 42.962 billion. There were only a few NRIs who were interested in sick units. The sick units thus attracted only Rs 1.237 billion of NRIs' investment.

Table 5.1 shows the amount of approved NRIs' investment. Let us now examine the actual inflow of funds on this account. It may be mentioned here that figures supplied by different governmental agencies vary widely. The SIA (Section for Industrial Approvals) Newsletter published by the Ministry of Industrial Development, Government of India shows that during January 1991–June 1999, the actual inflow was 98.9 per cent of the approved amount. However, the figures obtained from the NRIs, cell of the Indian Investment Centre, Government of India are different. Table 5.2, which

Table 5.1   Direct Investment Approval for NRIs

Amount in Rs million

	1984–91 annual average	1991–2	1992–3	1993–4	1994–5	1995–6	1996–7	1997–8	1998–9 (First 6 months)
A. Repatriable of which	2132.3	3182.2	18494.5	25172.7	59796.0	54440.6	65856.8	28504.8	4192.9
40% scheme	–	3106.1	17763.4	17682.3	43691.9	28232.7	15321.4	3914.3	625.4
74% scheme	–	10.9	–	–	–	–	–	–	–
100%automatic approval scheme	–	65.2	731.1	6847.9	10350.6	6050.0	14739.8	7905.6	1152.2
Real-estate development	–	–	–	180.1	1808.9	8590.1	20631.5	3382.5	1258.6
Air-taxi scheme	–	–	–	462.4	463.1	55.7	418.3	–	–
24% scheme	–	–	–	–	3481.5	11512.1	13797.7	13302.4	867.8
Sick units	–	–	–	–	–	–	948.1	–	288.9
B. Non-repatriable	405.4	47.0	9.9	–	–	–	–	–	–
Total (A+B)	2537.7	3229.2	18504.4	25172.7	59796.0	54440.6	65856.8	28504.8	4192.9

Source: Indian Investment Centre Documents.

is based on the figures of the Indian Investment Centre, shows a different picture. The figures are available on a calendar-year basis; and so, only an approximate ratio can be found between the approved amount and the actual inflow. Nevertheless, on the whole, during the period of reform, the actual investment inflow stood at around one-sixth of the approved amount. This ratio is not unusually low in the sense that it falls more or less in line with that in case of overall direct investment in the country during the first six years of reform (Sharan, 1998).

Table 5.2 also presents the sector-wise allocation of NRI direct investment during 1991–8. Repatriable investment, engineering items, and metals and their manufactures availed over one-sixth of the actual inflow. Another 6.18 per cent was availed by textiles. Medical equipment attracted 4.75 per cent of the investment inflow and over five per cent of the investment was claimed by electrical equipment. Food products and paper products claimed 3.53 per cent and 2.99 per cent respectively. The share of hotels, chemicals, and glass industry was collectively 7.51 per cent. This shows that repatriable investment was widely distributed among industries. But, on the other hand, non-repatriable investment was concentrated in a few industries. For example, food products alone accounted for a quarter of the inflow, followed by printing industry that claimed over one-eighth. This shows that a little less than two-fifths of such investment flowed to only two groups of industries. The other six industries, viz. chemicals, textiles, engineering, rubber goods, drugs and pharmaceuticals, and medical equipment were responsible for 14.94 per cent of such investment.

Portfolio Investment

For portfolio investment, figures were available only till 1993–4. These indicate that the magnitude of investment has risen during the period of reform. As far as repatriable investment is concerned, the pre-reform yearly average was Rs 45.2 million which, except for 1991–2, rose to Rs 295.8 million during 1992–3 and to Rs 474.6 million during 1993–4. The amount of non-repatriable investment was lower, but in this

Table 5.2   Actual Flow of Direct Investment of NRIs in Different Sectors
(Jan 1991–Dec 1998)

Amount in Rs million

Repatriable			Non-repatriable		
Sector/industry	Amount	% share	Sector/industry	Amount	% share
Engineering	3677.2	9.72	Food products	615.2	25.08
Metals	2914.0	7.71	Printing	302.6	12.36
Textiles	2340.5	6.18	Chemicals	150.9	6.15
Medical equipment	1798.8	4.75	Textiles	63.8	2.61
Electrical equipment	1920.4	5.08	Engineering	47.0	1.91
Food products	1335.0	3.53	Rubber goods	31.0	1.26
Paper products	1130.5	2.99	Drugs and Pharma	40.0	1.63
Hotels	1337.8	3.54	Medical equipment	33.9	1.38
Chemicals	833.9	2.21			
Glass	665.8	1.76			
Total incl. others	37813.1	100.00	Total incl. others	2451.8	100.00

Source: Indian Investment Centre documents.

case too, the size of investment in 1992–3 and 1993–4 was higher than the annual average in the pre-reform period.

Table 5.3   Portfolio Investment Approval

Amount in Rs million

Period	Repatriable	Non-repatriable
(Annual average) 1984–91	45.2	9.3
1991–2	32.0	4.0
1992–3	295.8	15.7
1993–4	474.6	18.4

Source: Indian Investment Centre documents.

Again, with the implementation of the Budget proposals for 1998–9, the ceiling for their investment in corporate securities rose. At the same time, there were UTI and SBI bonds specifically meant for their investment.

When we talk of SBI bonds, the question of RIBs issued in August 1998 in line with the announcement made in the Union Budget for 1998–9 cannot be overlooked. These bonds were meant for channelling funds from the NRIs and overseas corporate bodies (OCBs). The bonds were issued in three different currencies, viz. US dollar, pound sterling, and Deutschmark. The interest rate varied between 6.25 per cent and 8 per cent depending upon the denomination of currency and maturity after 5 years. The redemption was to be made in the currency of subscription. Interest could be paid either on a cumulative basis or on a bi-annual non-cumulative basis. The bonds were transferable among the NRIs or could be gifted to a resident only once with no transfers among the donees. Income from the RIBs was exempted from income tax, wealth tax and gift tax.

Total mobilization through RIBs amounted to an equivalent of $ 4.23 billion (RBI, 1999). This flow of funds occurred at a time when sanctions were imposed on India following the Pokharan nuclear test and when there were adverse sentiments in the international markets owing to downgrading of India's sovereign rating.

Company Deposits

The NRIs' deposits with the non-banking companies have been fluctuating widely. The figures in Table 5.4, which are on a calendar-year basis, show that in the pre-reform period, the sum of annual average of repatriable and non-repatriable deposits was equal to Rs 42.4 million. For the first two years of reform, that is during 1991 and 1992, the size of deposits squeezed to the range of Rs 11–14 million, but then the deposits increased and they were of the value of Rs 84.8 million during 1993. In 1993, repatriable deposit was larger, while in the previous two years non-repatriable deposit was larger. In 1994, the repatriable deposits increased, but there was net withdrawal of non-repatriable deposit. The result was that the addition to the total deposit was only a meagre Rs 16.1 million. During 1995 and 1996, there was net withdrawal of repatriable deposits, but there was minor addition to the non-repatriable deposits. The latter was small compared to the former with the result that total deposits turned negative. In 1997, both the types of deposits increased. But during the first six months of 1998, for which the figures are available, there occurred a huge withdrawal of repatriable as well as non-repatriable deposits by Rs 327.6 million. Owing to large

Table 5.4 NRI Deposits with Non-banking Companies

Amount in Rs million

Period	Repatriable	Non-repatriable	Total
Annual average (Sept 1983–Dec 1990)	28.1	14.3	42.4
1991	0.4	10.3	10.7
1992	1.3	13.1	14.4
1993	59.6	25.2	84.8
1994	127.3	–111.2	16.1
1995	–68.1	11.2	–56.9
1996	–80.1	15.8	–64.3
1997	11.4	45.8	57.2
Jan–Jun 1998	–235.7	–91.9	–327.6

Source: Indian Investment Centre documents.

withdrawals of deposits during the period of economic reform, the outstanding amount of such deposits at the end of June 1998 was barely Rs 41.6 million as compared to Rs 307.2 million at the end of December 1990 (IIC, 1999).

Bank Deposits

Compared to direct and portfolio investment, bank deposits by the NRIs have not fared well during the period of reform. In fact, the policy of the Indian Government has not been very stable. Two new foreign-currency deposit schemes were introduced, while two such schemes were withdrawn. To be precise, FCNR account, which had attracted huge deposits during pre-reform period, say, equivalent of Rs 18.3 billion annually between 1984-5 and 1990-1 (Sharan, 1993), did not do well during the period of reform. In the very first fiscal year of the reform period, there was a net withdrawal from the deposits. Except for 1992-3, there was continual net withdrawal. Moreover, the RBI had to pay a high price by way of exchange guarantees. All these were the reasons for withdrawal of this scheme. By July 1998, the entire deposit was withdrawn. The FCNR(O) (ordinary) account, which was introduced in November, 1990, attracted only a meagre deposit for $ 1044 million till 1992-3, but then there was a net withdrawal and the account was closed. Presently, there is only one foreign currency account, FCNR(B) (bank) account where RBI does not shoulder the exchange rate guarantee. The deposits under this scheme fared well up to 1995-6 as the quantum of annual deposit rose from $ 1108 million in 1993-4 to $ 2657 million during 1995-6, but then it slowed down to $ 1776 million in 1996-7 and to $ 971 million in 1997-8. In 1998-9, there was a net withdrawal of $ 144 million from this account.

In the case of the non-resident rupee account, the size of deposits has not been very impressive. In NRER account, there was a net withdrawal of deposits in 1991-2 and 1992-3, but there were also fresh deposits in the following two fiscal years. Again, there was net withdrawal in 1995-6, but then there were fresh deposits. The amount of fresh deposits went on continual decline from the 1996-7 level and it continued till

Table 5.5 Bank Deposits by NRIs

Amount in million $

Schemes	Outstanding by March 1991	1991–2	1992–3	1993–4	1994–5	1995–6	1996–7	1997–98	1998–9	Outstanding on 1 April 1999
FCNR	10103	–311	825	–1317	–2249	–2796	–1949	–2270	–36	0
FCNR(B)				1108	1955	2657	1776	971	–144	8323
FCNR(O)	262	345	437	–511	–533	–	–	–	–	0
NRER	3618	–593	–85	783	1033	–640	1067	654	383	6220
NRNRR			621	1133	732	1056	2062	658	496	6758

Source: 1. Government of India, (1997) *Economic Survey 1996–7* New Delhi: Ministry of Finance.
2. Reserve Bank of India, (1999) *Annual Report 1998–9* Bombay.

1998–9. In NRNRR account, the amount of deposit fluctuated form $ 621 million in 1992-3 to $ 1133 million in 1993-4, to $ 732 million in 1994-5 and to $ 1056 million in 1995-6. In 1996-7, it was over two billion US dollars, but again, it dropped to $ 658.0 million in 1997-8 and to $ 496 million during 1998-9.

Conclusion

NRIs do have a contribution in the strengthening of India's external balance. Because of a host of incentives provided to them during the period of reform, their investment registered an upward move, although since 1997-8, it has come down. Direct investment has been far larger than the portfolio investment. Similarly, repatriable investment has been far greater than the non-repatriable one.

Direct investment has not necessarily been guided by the extent of their participation in the equity of Indian companies. It is because the investment under the 100 per cent scheme is smaller than under the 40 per cent scheme. In the 100 per cent scheme, it is mainly the high-priority industrial sector that has availed the largest segment of invesetment. The 24 per cent scheme too has availed growing size of investment. But the sick units have failed to attract investment.

The sectoral allocation of direct investment shows that repatriable investment is widely distributed over different industries. On the other hand, the non-repatrable investment is concentrated over a few industries.

NRIs showed interest in non-banking company deposits during the earlier part of the reform period, then as a result of net withdrawal, the outstanding amount of such deposits sagged considerably. The bank deposit both in foreign-currency and rupee accounts has not fared well during the period of reform. Thus, in short, greater liberalization duing the period of reform has definitely helped attract greater volume of NRIs' investment, although the emerging picture is not completely an unmixed one.

6

Foreign Portfolio Investment

The economic reform measures to strengthen the external sector, did not remain confined to encouraging FDI alone. A new door was opened in 1992 to stimulate inflow of foreign exchange when the Indian Government allowed foreign portfolio investment (FPI) to flow into the country. In the following years, the norms for FPI were liberalized to boost such flows. The purpose of the present chapter is to examine whether this new move has helped increase the quantum of the foreign-exchange inflow into the country. In the beginning, it discusses different forms of FPI and the policy of the Indian Government; and then, it examines the impact of the liberal policy on the size of the investment inflow.

Channels for the Flow of FPI

There are a few channels for the flow of FPI. In one, foreign investors, normally the foreign institutional investors (FIIs) such as investment companies, mutual funds etc., involve themselves in sale and purchase of corporate securities at the stock exchange in India. The excess of purchase amount over the sale amount represents the inflow of foreign capital.

In the other mode, an Indian company sells its securities — shares and convertible debentures — in the international capital market under American Depository Receipt (ADR) or Global Depository Receipt (GDR) mechanism. After getting the green signal from government authorities, the security-issuing company deposits its shares with a custodian bank in India. The latter instructs the overseas depository bank to issue a negotiable instrument in the form of a depository receipt against the shares held by it (the custodian bank). ADR is issued in US dollars, while GDR is issued in any convertible currency and is listed on an international stock exchange.

The investment flows from the purchaser of depository receipt to the depository abroad, from depository to the custodian bank, and finally, from the custodian bank to the issuing company. Such issues, usually known as Euro-issues, are not allowed to exceed 51 per cent of the issued and subscribed capital of the issuing company.

The conversion of foreign-currency convertible bonds (FCCB) does not give rise to any capital gain liable to any tax in India. A GDR can be cancelled by sending it back to the custodian in India. In this case, the issuing company releases multiples of GDR share certificates that are sold in the domestic market by local brokers. The proceeds from sales are remitted to the custodian who gets them converted into foreign currency, and after deducting the capital gains tax, remits the funds back to investor through its own counter-part abroad.

Besides these two main channels, there are some offshore funds and proceeds from the issues of floating rate notes, etc. that too form a part of FPI. Such inflows have been sizeable ascending from $ 5 million in 1992–3 to $ 382 million in 1993–4, but then plummeting to $ 239 million in 1994–5, $ 56 million in 1995–6 and to $ 20 million 1996–7. During 1997–8, it revived to $ 204 million but again dropped to $ 59 million during 1998–9 (see Table 6.2).

Reasons for Choosing FPI

The Indian Government was not the first to choose the FPI route. In many developing countries, this route had helped bring in large amounts of foreign exchange. Statistics show that FPI into developing countries had increased phenomenally from $ 3.5 billion in 1989 to $ 8.2 billion in 1992 (International Finance Corporation, 1993). The Indian Government simply followed suit.

Secondly, allowing FPI served the very objective of globalization of the economy. The Indian capital market came in close link with international investors that helped the former to become more competitive.

Thirdly, Indian companies derived benefits from low interest rates prevailing in the international capital market. This in turn made them more cost-competitive inasmuch as the financing cost is a major segment of the total cost.

Fourthly, the operation of FIIs at the stock exchange was expected to improve the performance standard of the country's stock exchanges. It is often argued that when the FIIs increase their demand for shares, share prices go up. It gives a boost to new issues. But if the FIIs lower their demand or sell the securities, share prices fall. The fall in share prices leads to greater sale of securities by the FIIs. A vicious circle starts and the balance of payments is adversely affected. But such a case has not been very common. In the past five years, it is only since November 1997 that FIIs' net investment has frequently been in the negative zone.

When India launched this scheme, the FIIs were found to be very interested in the Indian capital market. This was because some 'push' factors were operating. The developing markets ranked high among the best performing markets and so the investors expected high returns from India too (Shrivastawa, 1997). Moreover, the decline in the interest rate in the OECD (Organization of Economic Cooperation and Development) countries during the 1990s motivated those investors to turn to India and other developing countries.

Their operation in India or other developing countries helped them to diversify their investment portfolio that considerably lessened their investment risk (Meric and Meric, 1989). So it was high return cum lower risk that motivated the FIIs to invest in India.

Measures of FPI Policy Reform

Euro-issues

According to the guidelines notified by the Government of India in regard to Euro-issues, a company going for Euro-issues has to obtain prior permission from the Government. The first guideline clearly stated that only those companies that had possessed good track record for at least three years could make Euro-issues. Moreover, the policy never stressed on the lock-in period. (GOI, 1993).

The second guideline was issued in May 1994 according to which an Indian company could not float the Euro-issue more than once a year. There was also a provision for selective retention of Euro-issue proceeds abroad that could be used either for import of capital goods or for retiring foreign-currency debt or for capitalizing joint-ventures abroad. The companies were to submit a report about the use of such funds (The Economic Times, 12 May 1994).

In October 1994, it was made mandatory to keep money abroad till the actual utilization of proceeds. Moreover, the funds were to be used not necessarily within one year. This was done to avoid haste in the using of funds. The companies were allowed to park their funds in stock market or in the shape of real estate abroad. The coverage of issuers was broadened to also include the select financial institutions that could go for Euro-issues on behalf of small and medium-scale companies. However, the issue of warrants along with GDR was banned (The Economic Times, 14 October 1994).

In June 1996, the guidelines were further liberalized. The requirements for consistently good performance for three years were relaxed if the Euro-issues were meant for the infrastructure sector. The restrictions on the number of issues to be floated by a company during a particular financial year were withdrawn. The norms regarding end-use of GDR proceeds were relaxed to include financing of capital-goods imports, capital expenditure regarding installation of plant, software development, etc. Using up to one quarter of GDR proceeds for meeting working capital requirements was permitted. For banks, financial institutions and non-banking financial companies, the end-use clause was not obligatory. However, the investment of GDR proceeds in stock market and real estate was prohibited (GOI, 1997).

In May 1998, the guidelines were further relaxed. Unlisted companies maintaining a three-year track record of performance could go for Euro-issues. This opened the door for all greenfield projects, most of which are unlisted, to access the international capital markets. The other point was that the Euro-equities were treated as full-risk equity; and so, all end-use restrictions on such proceeds were removed. But this was not the case with the FCCBs (Business Standard, 23 May 1998).

In August 1998, the Indian Government allowed Indian companies to issue bonus shares or right shares to the GDR/ADR holders after obtaining necessary permission. Moreover, the 90-day validity period for final approvals of ADR/GDR issues was withdrawn making the approval valid even thereafter. This is expected to bring in greater flexibility as regards the timing of issues.

FIIs' Investment

The first guideline issued in September 1992 permitted the FIIs to operate at the stock exchanges subject to their registration with SEBI and approval from the RBI. There was, of course, a ceiling on their investment. A company could sell up to a maximum of 24 per cent of the issued shares. The share of a particular FII was not to exceed 5 per cent of the issued share capital in an Indian company. The FIIs were to allocate their total investment between equities and debentures in the ratio of 70:30. They could enjoy a concessional tax rate of 20 per cent on dividend and interest and of 10 per cent on long-term capital gains.

In the following year, the tax rate on short-term capital gains was fixed at 30 per cent. At the same time, foreign brokers were allowed to operate in India on behalf of the FIIs. Previously, the FIIs' funds were channelled through foreign banks serving as custodians.

The Budget proposals for 1997–8 raised the ceiling for FIIs' investment in a company from 24 per cent to 30 per cent of the issued capital. Subsequently, the FIIs were allowed to invest even in the securities of unlisted companies and in the treasury bills and gilt-edged government securities. The Proprietary Funds were also allowed to make investment in the country through the FII-route. The norms for FIIs' investment in convertible bonds were also liberalized subject to specific guidelines. The Budget proposals for 1997–8 too emphasized on FIIs' investment in unlisted securities.

Now transactions among the FIIs with reference to Indian stocks will no longer require post-facto confirmation from the RBI. Moreover, 100 per cent FII debt funds have been permitted to invest in unlisted debt securities of the Indian companies. Moreover, authorized dealers in the foreign-exchange market have been permitted to provide forward cover to FIIs in respect of their fresh equity investments in the country.

Magnitude of Investment

Euro-issues

The first Euro-issue dates back to May 1992 when Reliance Industries issued shares for $ 150 million. It was followed by another issue for $ 90 million by Grasim Industries in November that year. These were the two issues during 1992–3. In 1993–4, there were 17 issues of equity for $ 1597 million and 9 issues of FCCBs for $ 896 million. In 1994–5, the amount of Euro-equities was still larger crossing $ 2 billion, but the Government approved FCCB issue only for $ 102 million (Table 6.1). In fact, this restriction aimed at containing external indebtedness from rising.

In 1995–6, only Euro-equities were issued and that too for only $ 627 million. There was, of course, revival in 1996–7 when there were six cases of Euro-equity issue for $ 1.4 billion, accompanied by three cases of FCCB issue for $ 448 million. But in 1997–8, there was only one issue of equities and the approved amount was barely $ 359 million. The figure about the issues during 1998–9 was the minimal as there was only one issue of Euro-equities and that too for only $ 70 million (Table 6.1). The far lower size of issue during 1997–8 and 1998–9 can be attributed to a downward trend in industrial activities in the country which was reflected in the falling growth rate of industrial production. The statistics show that the growth rate of industrial production was barely 6.6 per cent and 4 per cent respectively in these two years as compared to 8.4 per cent in 1994–5 and 12.7 per cent in 1995–6 (RBI, 1999). Moreover, there was a bearish trend in the

Indian capital market either as a result of lower industrial activities at home or because of various economic problems prevailing in the global economy. The bearish trend in the capital market is explained at some length in the following section.

Table 6.1 also shows the actual flow of funds on this count. The actual inflow was, of course, low at 36 per cent of the approved amount during 1992-3, but then this percentage (cumulative flow as percentage of cumulative approval) increased sharply to 62 in 1993-4, 72 in 1994-5 and 75 in 1995-6. After dropping slightly to 70 during 1996-7, the actual flow as percentage of the approved amount (on a cumulative basis) moved up again to 75 in 1997-8 and further to 78 during 1998-9.

When this percentage is compared with the actual inflow of foreign direct investment as a percentage of the approved amount, foreign portfolio investment on account of Euro-issues fares far better. It is because in case of foreign direct investment, actual inflow as percentage of approved investment has been much lower (as shown in Table 4.1).

FIIs' Investment

Despite the fact that the entry of FIIs was cleared by the Government in September 1992, their investment amounting to $ 1 million occurred only in the last quarter of the fiscal year, 1992-3. Subsequently, greater number of FIIs showed interest in the Indian capital market. Foreign brokers were also allowed to operate helping FII operation on a larger scale. As a result, the size of net investment jumped up to $ 1665 million during 1993-4. After a meagre drop to $ 1503 million in 1994-5, it rose again to over $ 2 billion during 1995-6. It fell marginally to $ 1926 million during 1996-7 but then fell fast to $ 979 million in 1997-8. During 1998-9, it was FIIs' disinvestment that stood at $ 390 million (Table 6.2). In fact, the disinvestment had started in November 1997 which continued to exist almost every month till November 1998.

Thus there have been ups and downs in the FIIs' net investment. In fact, the investors in the capital market are fair weather friends. When macroeconomic and political

Table 6.1 Euro-issues: Approval and Actual Flow

Amount in $ million

Year	Issue of Euro-equities		Issue of FCCBs		Total amount of Euro-issue	Amount of actual flow	Actual Flow as % approved amount
	No.	Amount	No.	Amount			
1992–3	2	240	—	—	240	86	36
1993–4	17	1597	9	896	2493	1602	62
1994–5	28	2050	2	102	2152	1839	72
1995–6	7	627	—	—	627	683	75
1996–7	6	1407	3	448	1855	918	70
1997–8	1	359	–	–	359	645	75
1998–9	1	70	–	–	70	270	78
Total	62	6350	14	1446	7796	6043	

Note: The last column shows the cumulative flow as percentage of cumulative approvals.

Sources: 1. For approvals up to 1996–7, Tata Services, (1997) *Statistical Outline of India, 1997–8*, Bombay: Department of Economics and Statistics, p. 138.

2. For 1997–9 figures, *The Economic Times*, 17 June 1998 and 16 November 1999.

3. For actual flow up to 1996–7, RBI, (1997) *Report on Currency and Finance 1996–7*, Bombay, p. 181.

4. For 1997–8 figures, Government of India, (1998) *Economic Survey 1997–8*, New Delhi: Ministry of Finance, p. 87.

5. For 1998–9 figures, RBI, (1999) *Annual Report 1998–9*, Bombay.

indicators behave well, there is large demand for securities. On the other hand, when the economic downtrend is visible or there are political disturbances, the demand for securities falls fast and investors begin selling them. Since the FIIs dominate the Indian stock market, their purchase and sale of securities greatly influence the stock-market index. Sometimes a vicious circle is created which needs some explanation. During improved economic and political conditions, investors expect a rise in the industrial profitability as a result of which they buy securities. The purchase of securities leads to an increase in their demand and their prices. This raises the stock-market index. Again, with an increase in the stock-market index, there is a bullish trend that leads to greater purchase of securities and an increase in their prices at the stock market. However, with deterioration in economic and political conditions, a reverse trend of falling demand for securities and falling stock-market index begins. There may be day-to-day fluctuations, but the trend continues for some time.

The FIIs' investment in India too was the victim of the changing economic and political scenario. Till 1996-7, the size of net investment was large because the macroeconomic fundamentals were stronger. There was also political stability in the country on account of the ruling party enjoying absolute majority in parliament. But thereafter, there was a drastic fall in investments in 1997-8 and 1998-9. This particular downtrend was the outcome of various factors that need some explanation here. First of all, it was the political instability. A coalition government had already been formed in which the left parties, which opposed some of the economic reform measures, were the members. Moreover, the government was dependent on the wishes of the Congress party, as a result of which its life was unpredictable. The Prime Minister was changed at the behest of the Congress party which added to further political instability. In 1998, the Bhartiya Janata Party Government took office but it too was a fragile government as some of the coalition partners were attempting to destabilize the government.

Besides political instability, the economic downtrend at home was another factor dampening FIIs' investment. As discussed, the annual growth rate of industrial production was 6.6 per cent and 4 per cent during 1997–8 and 1998–9 compared to 8.4 per cent in 1994–5 and as high as 12.7 per cent in 1995–6 (RBI, 1999).

Factors operating abroad also had an impact on the FIIs' investment at the Indian stock exchanges. There was a marked fall in the world economic growth rate during 1997 and 1998. Moreover, the Russian default on government debt and the consequent devaluation of the rouble, recession in Japan, collapse of the crawling peg system of exchange rate in Brazil, and more importantly the financial crisis in South-East Asian countries were some of the factors that caused a dampening investment climate on the world economic map. The long-term and short-term capital flows to developing countries were found depressed (RBI, 1999; United Nations, 1999). India was no exception and so disinterestedness among the FIIs operating at the Indian stock exchanges was not a surprise.

In this context, it may be reiterated that the crisis in the South-East Asian countries had a greater impact on the Indian capital market in view of a close link between these economies and the Indian economy either through trade or the investment. The link came to be stronger in view of openness of the Indian economy in the wake of the economic reforms. The crisis began in the second quarter of 1997 and turned serious since mid-1997 through mid 1998. The FIIs operating at the global level might have visualized that the seriousness of the crisis might hurt the Indian securities market. Hence they began selling their securities at the Indian stock exchanges. As a result, the securities market index in India began falling – from 1191.9 in August 1997 to 959.5 in February 1998 (1980–1 = 100). After improvement for a couple months, it again began falling and reached 907.7 by October 1998 (RBIB, 1999). The sale of securities in bulk by them further depressed the stock-market index and the depressed index caused further sale of securities by them. The entire period ranging from November 1997 to November 1998, except March 1998, witnessed a net disinvestment on the FIIs' account ranging between $ 31 million and $ 276 million per month (RBIB, 1999). Though South-East Asian crisis was not solely responsible for the net disinvestment, the presence of this factor cannot be denied.

Conclusion

After discussing the different components of portfolio investment in India, it would be appropriate to depict an overall position so as to assess the contribution of FPI to strengthening of the balance of payments. Table 6.2 shows that its size ascended from a figure of $ 92 million in 1992–3 to over $ 3.6 billion in the following fiscal year, 1993–4. The level of investment remained constant in 1994–5. However, it plummeted to $ 2.7 billion in 1995–6 owing to a high degree of contraction in the flow on account of Euro-issues. In 1996–7, the revival of Euro-issue proceeds led the total portfolio investment to surge up to $ 2.9 billion, but again, owing to sluggishness both on account of FIIs' investment and Euro-issue flow, the size of portfolio investment got slashed to $ 1.8 billion in 1997–8. During 1998–9, owing to net disinvestment on FIIs' account and only a meagre inflow on other counts, the FPI inflow remained negative by $ 61 million (Table 6.2).

A comparative picture of different segments of FPI shows that commencing from 1993–94, every fiscal year except for 1994–5 and 1998–9, the size of FIIs' investment (net) was larger than the Euro-issue proceeds. The other inflows on portfolio investment account were obviously not significant.

When one compares FPI inflow with FDI inflow, a couple of facts are evident. One is that the former has been more volatile than the latter. But this is nothing unique with India where like in other developing countries, the annual fluctuation in FPI flow has been more than that in case of FDI flow. The statistics reveal that during 1992–7, the co-efficient of variation in the foreign portfolio investment flow into developing countries was 0.43 compared to 0.35 in case of foreign direct investment flow. In some of the Asian developing countries attracting large flow of foreign investment, annual fluctuation in FPI has been much larger than that in FDI (United Nations, 1998).

The other fact is that between 1992–3 and 1998–9, FPI flow in India has been higher than FDI inflow (Reserve Bank of India Bulletin, September 1999). This indicates the significance of the contribution of FPI in strengthening India's balance of payments.

Table 6.2   Foreign Portfolio Investment

Amount in $ million

	1992-3	1993-4	1994-5	1995-6	1996-7	1997-8	1998-9	Total
Euro-issues	86	1602	1839	683	918	645	270	6043
FIIs' investment	1	1665	1503	2009	1926	979	-390	7693
Offshore funds	5	382	239	56	20	204	59	965
Total	92	3649	3581	2748	2864	1828	-61	14701

Sources: 1. For figures up to 1996-7, RBI, (1997) *Report on Currency and Finance 1996-7*, Bombay.
2. For 1997-8 figures, Government of India, (1998) *Economic Survey 1997-8*, New Delhi: Ministry of Finance.
3. For 1998-9 figures, RBI, (1999) *Annual Report 1998-9*, Bombay.

There is, of course, a question whether the portfolio investment in India has been at par with the international standards. Shrivastwa (1997) has made a comparative study and finds that India does lag but not far behind. It is only next to Latin American and a few other countries. As far as growth in such investment is concerned, the net portfolio investment in developing countries, according to Shrivastwa, soared up from $ 6 billion in 1990 to $ 92 billion in 1996, that is over 15-fold. In India, this increase was marked from $ 92 million in 1992-3 to $ 2.9 billion in 1996-7, although a drop in it was marked in the following period.

In short, the policy of liberalization and globalization under the aegis of macroeconomic reform in India has been a stimulant for large inflow of FPI into the country that has in turn helped strengthen the external sector.

7

India's Overseas Investment

One of the measures to strengthen the external sector under the aegis of macroeconomic reforms in India has centred on promoting the country's overseas investment. The policy of the Indian Government on this count turned more encouraging and more transparent for the first time in October 1992 which was followed by further relaxation in subsequent years. Now the question is whether liberalization in this area has paid a substantial dividend. The present discussion offers an answer to this question. It embraces, among other things, the rationale behind this measure of the Indian Government, the broad features of the investment overseas and the contribution of such investment to the country's balance of payments.

Rationale behind the Internationalization of Indian Firms

There was a time when the multinational firms were headquartered in the industrialized countries, but since the mid-1960s and more especially since 1970s, they also came to be headquartered in the developing countries. One group of developing countries was represented by some of the oil-exporting countries that acquired huge foreign exchange in the wake of the international oil price rise. With a command over the supply of oil and after the acquisition of technology, the firms thereof went mostly for vertical operations in energy projects abroad (Rosenbaum and Tyler, 1975).

To the other group, belonged the industrializing countries of the developing world that had been importing technology from the industrialized world. After the import of technology for a long period, they were in a position to export the imported technology either after modification or even without any modification. India belongs to this second group.

Most of the theories that had explained the internationalization of firms in developed countries are applicable to some extent in case of firms in developing countries. For example, Hymer's (1976) organizational theory could well be explained in case of the developing countries' multinationals. It is quite evident that primarily those firms of the industrializing developing countries that possess some kind of 'firm-specific' or 'ownership' advantage, either in the form of modified technology more suitable for the other developing countries or in the form of innovated product, have moved abroad. There are two types of modification that they have adopted. One is the scale-down modification, economizing the cost of production that is more suitable for the consumption pattern in the developing countries. The other is the scale-up modification allowing product sophistication that is suitable for the consumption pattern in the developed countries. In fact, this is the reason that firms of the developing world have moved not only to other developing countries but also to the developed countries.

The movement of the developing countries' firms to the industrialized world is nothing unique. The 'International Product Life Cycle' phenomenon clearly exhibits how such investment takes place after the products have gone a full circle (Wells, 1969). Wen-lee Ting (1982) has cited the case of Tatung Company of Taiwan which imported technology from the US and Japan for the manufacture of household appliances and electronic items, and after successful employment of technology, it moved to set up affiliates in the US and Japan.

In the Indian context, it is quite evident that firms have long been importing improved technology from the industrialized world and over the decades they have been able to bring about desired modifications in technology. As a result, they have come to possess the firm-specific advantage that encourages them to operate abroad.

Besides technology the firm-specific advantage of the Indian firms has also enhanced managerial capabilities of the Indians. Sanjay Lall (1982) finds that around three- fourths of Indian overseas investment in the early 1980s were handled by seven large industrialists who had a long standing in managing the concerns and who could well compete with those of the developed countries.

The locational theory developed by Hood and Young (1979) is also applicable to the internationalization of the developing countries' firms in general and the Indian firms in particular. This theory explains that a firm moves abroad to exploit cheap and abundant raw material or to exploit cheap labour force. If we glance at the Indian firms, it is quite evident that some of them have moved to Sri Lanka for the manufacture of rubber products because of easy availability of rubber in that country. Indian firms have moved to Bangladesh for the manufacture of paper and paper products and to Nepal for medicinal (herbal) preparations in view of easy availability of raw material. There are many such examples.

Raymond Vernon's (1966, 1979) product cycle theory of the behaviour of multinational corporations is also applicable to Indian firms going international. Vernon explains this operation in different stages. First, the firm exports the innovated product to other countries. But then, when the demand for that product becomes mature in the importing countries and when the competitors producing similar products appear in those countries, the product does not remain price-inelastic. The firm, in order to compete with the local competitors in the importing countries, sets up its own manufacturing unit there because this way it is able to avoid transportation cost and tariff. In India too, the firms imported technology, manufactured new types of goods and exported them to other developing countries. It was possible because the technology they imported was normally meant for a larger market and also because the Indian government permitted technology import on the grounds that the technology-importing firm would export a significant portion of the output. After being exported for some time, the products became mature and the exporting firm preferred to set up its own manufacturing unit in the importing countries. This explanation appears valid in the Indian context when firms moved to foreign countries only after a long period of manufacturing with imported technology. Indian technology and products were preferred by other developing countries insofar as the modified technology was more suitable. Moreover, Indian firms supplied to them at more favourable terms (Sharan, 1985). The operation of Indian firms was not limited to the developing world, some of them also moved to the industrialized world, especially when the modified technology was appreciated and demanded there.

Besides the theoretical rationale for the internationalization of Indian firms, there are many other factors responsible for such a move. The issue of improvement in the balance of payments is the most important. Internationalization of Indian firms involves initially an outflow of foreign exchange in form of investment, but this does not pose as serious a problem as repatriation of dividend or royalty and technical service fees back to India compensates the loss of foreign exchange. This is particularly true where one of the conditions behind approval of joint-ventures abroad is that the investment in cash normally has to be balanced through the repatriation of dividend within a period of five years. Any repatriation of dividend over and above the value of investment outflow improves the invisible earnings on investment income account and thereby cuts the current account deficit. Thus from this angle promoting joint ventures abroad was an indispensable step to salvage the investment income account which was badly distressed during the early 1990s owing to external debt servicing.

Promotion of joint ventures helps augment export. Investment is in cash and kind though in the Indian case, investment in kind has always been larger than the investment in cash. Investment in kind takes the form of plant and machinery and other components. Thus promoting joint-ventures and thereby a larger investment in kind was a right step during the period of reform to axe huge trade deficit that was prevalent during the early 1990s.

Firms move abroad with a view to exploit cheap and abundant raw material in the host country. Such a move pushes down the cost of production and makes the firm competitive in the international market. Exports increase and in turn the balance of payments improves. The argument fits well in the Indian case·as this factor has been present in many cases.

Again, it is often found that technicians accompany the export of technology. It is more common in the case of project export and turn-key jobs. When Indian technicians go abroad, they often send a part of their income back home to their family. This inflates the remittances that form a part of invisible earnings. This may have been one of the factors behind promoting joint ventures abroad.

Against this backdrop, it can safely be said that Indian firms possess the necessary strength for going international. They have a long experience of over three decades. It was during the mid-1960s when Indian firms began moving abroad and by 1981–2, there were over 465 approvals for foreign joint-ventures. They were spread over 26 countries and were engaged in manufacturing as well as non-manufacturing activities (Sharan, 1985). If the Indian Government decided to encourage overseas investment in 1992, it was a right step as the Indian firms possessed the requisite base.

Measures of Overseas Investment Policy Reform

The policy of liberalization that was initiated in October 1992 aimed *inter alia* at a couple of aspects, such as simplification of the procedural formalities and the raising of the ceiling for investment in the form of cash. It provided for automatic approval of overseas investment if the amount of investment was within $ 2 million and the cash component thereof did not exceed $ 0.5 million. Such proposals were to be cleared within 30 days. Thus it was a major breakthrough towards easing of procedural formalities. The ceiling for cash investment was raised through another policy pronouncement in August 1995. The 1995 policy compartmentalized the proposals into two categories: 'fast track' and 'normal track'. The extent of cash investment and the procedural formalities were different in the two cases.

The fast-track cases involved automatic approval by the RBI within three weeks. Only those proposals qualified for the fast track where the following conditions were met:

- investment did not exceed $ 4 million although in case of rupee investment in Nepal, the limit was Rs 250 million
- the amount of investment was up to one quarter of the annual average of exports during past three years
- investment outflow was to be fully repatriated through dividend and other such remittances within a period of five years.

The investment might be entirely in cash or partly in the form of cash and partly as the value of plant and machinery supplied or of the payments for technology supplied.

The fast-track provisions also covered financial-sector joint ventures. But in this case, the proponent was required to have:

- a good track record for a minimum of three years
- got itself registered with the SEBI
- a net worth of Rs 150 million
- maintained a capital adequacy norm of 8 per cent

There was, of course, one limitation with the fast-track cases. Any Indian company could use this route only once in a block of three financial years.

The proposals not qualifying for the fast track automatically came under the 'normal track'. Under its ambit came proposals involving over $ 4 million but not exceeding $ 15 million. They were judged by a special committee which examined their feasibility in terms of foreign-exchange earnings and if satisfied, recommended them for RBI approval. However, as per the 1997 amendment, the proposals came to be approved even without reference to the RBI, if the Indian company maintained an EEFC account and if the balance in this account was sufficient. The August 1998 notification of the Government relaxed the condition further that the proposals might be approved even if sufficient balances did not exist in the EEFC account. Again, if the amount of investment came through the GDR route, any reference to the RBI was not required. The proposals were cleared by the Ministry of Finance. In November 1998, the

Government brought all foreign investment proposals involving an investment up to $ 15 million under the fast-track approval scheme.

It does not, however, mean that proposals involving an amount of investment exceeding $ 15 million are not permitted. They are cleared if the excess amount over and above $ 15 million comes through the GDR route. There are also cases of approval where the investment exceeds $ 15 million and the excess amount does not come through the GDR route, but they are very rare when the performance record of the proponent is exceptionally good.

The 1997 amendment also provides that if the investment up to $ 15 million is financed by the EEFC account or by GDR finances, the condition relating to the repatriation of investment such as through dividends within a specific period, does not apply. The scope of this provision has come to be wider since January 1999. Now the requirements of foreign-exchange neutrality in the form of dividend, royalty, etc. within a period of five years stand waived in all the cases of joint ventures and wholly-owned subsidiaries (WOS).

The cases of investment in SAARC member countries came to be preferentially treated. The investment proposal involving up to Rs 250 million and meant for Nepal came to be processed under the fast-track scheme. This ceiling was raised from Rs 250 million to Rs 600 million in August 1998 and investment in Bhutan was also brought within its ambit. Under the same notification, the ceiling meant for fast-track processing was raised from $ 4 million to $ 15 million for investment in other SAARC member countries. In May 1999, it was raised to Rs 1200 million in case of investment in Nepal and Bhutan and to $ 30 million in case of other SAARC member countries.

Size and Pattern of Overseas Investment

Magnitude of Investment

India has a long history of making overseas investment dating back to the mid-1960s. During the 1970s and 1980s, there were a large number of approvals for setting up of joint ventures abroad. But since the policy was contained within the ambit of the then existing FERA, it was not very liberal and failed to give a big push to investment overseas. At the end of 1991, there were only 245 ventures overseas, of which 161 were in operation and 84 were under different stages of implementation. Total investment in the equity of foreign concerns stood at Rs 1.209 billion or $ 49.4 million at the then existing exchange rate (GOI, 1993). Very few of the ventures represented investment in WOSs. This was perhaps because of a strict ceiling over investment in cash form.

But with the liberalization policy, there occurred an upward jump in the number of approved cases. At the same time, there was a phenomenal upsurge in the approval of investment in WOSs. The apparent result was that at the end of December 1995, the non-WOSs were as many as 593 of which 185 were in operation and the rest 408 were under different stages of implementation. Besides, there were 423 WOSs, out of which 81 were in operation and 342 were under implementation. Thus, the total number of overseas ventures rose to 1016, four times that   in 1991. What is revealing is that only 61 out of 423 WOSs were approved prior to October 1992 when the first move towards liberalization was afoot. The rest were approved only thereafter (IIC, 1998a).

The next three years witnessed faster growth. To be more specific, 146 WOSs were approved during 1996, although the number was slightly lower at 122 in 1997 and 132 in 1998. In addition, the number of approvals of non-WOSs during these three years was 112, 102 and 103 respectively. When we club together the number of approvals during these three years, the annual average is greater than that during 1992–5. This is 239 as compared to 193 during 1992–5. Moreover, there is a definite preference for WOSs in recent years. Even among the non-WOSs, those involving a greater percentage of Indian equity are sufficiently large. At the end of December 1995, there were 593 such ventures of which 273 involved Indian equity at 50 per cent or more. In 1997, 66 out of 102 ventures were approved with Indian equity participation being 50 per cent or more (IIC, 1998a).

With a clear inclination towards greater equity participation, it is but natural for the amount of overseas investment to largely grow during the liberalization period. Statistics show that from a meagre level of Rs 1.209 billion at the end of December 1991, the magnitude of overseas investment rose to Rs 33.620 billion at the end of December 1995. The amount at 1995-end was Rs 15.865 billion as investment in WOSs abroad and Rs. 17.755 billion in non-WOSs. This way, the average per annum addition to overseas investment during 1992–5 was of the order of Rs 8.103 billion. The figures for 1996 onwards are available in terms of US dollars. However, on converting them into Indian rupees, the amount of approval stood at Rs 8.328 billion in 1996 and Rs 18.772 billion in 1997 (IIC, 1998a). In 1998, there was a marginal drop in the approved investment overseas as the amount came down to Rs 6.199 billion. Nevertheless, the overall trend during the period of reform is positive showing a favourable impact of liberalized policy.

There is, of course, a question whether India's overseas investments have been comparable with that of some Asian developing countries. The statistics reveal that the annual average of the FDI outflow from India during 1992–7 has been worth $ 101 million compared to $ 20.8 billion from Hong Kong, $ 3.6 billion from Singapore, $ 3.2 billion from Malaysia and $ 3.0 billion from Korea during the same period (United Nations, 1998). Among the 50 largest multinationals from the developing world, there is only one Indian multinational, whereas this number is far more in case of some other developing countries of Asia. Thus the process of economic reforms still has a long way to go.

Geographic Pattern

Indian companies have reached different corners of the globe. WOSs are spread over 62 countries and non-WOSs have covered 86 countries. Since some of the host countries, especially the developing ones, do not allow 100 per cent equity participation by foreign companies, the coverage of the WOSs is smaller.

The statistics presented in Table 7.1 reveal that the Indian ventures have gone both to the developed and the developing world. In case of the WOSs abroad, the share of the developed countries at the end of December 1998 stood at 58.3 per cent. But in case of the non-WOSs, their share was only 30.9 per cent. Such a picture is due to the fact that the developed countries do not often mind 100 per cent equity participation by foreign companies.

It is evident from the Table 7.1 that in the case of the WOSs abroad, there is greater geographic concentration. Two countries, the US and the UK, account for three-fourths of the ventures directed to the developed world. The other four countries, viz. Germany, Russia, the Netherlands, and Switzerland account for 15.5 per cent. This means that these six countries account for 92 per cent of the total number of WOSs directed to the developed world. As far as developing countries are concerned, the geographic concentration is lower as two countries, Singapore and Mauritius, share only one-half of the WOSs moving to the developing world. Hong Kong, UAE and Sri Lanka claim another one-fifth.

Again, in case of non-WOSs, the US and the UK share over three-fifths of those moving to the developed world. Other two, Russia and Germany, share another one-fifth. In case of those moving to the developing world, concentration is not indicated as the share of any individual country is hardly 10 per cent or so.

Sectoral Pattern

The figures in Table 7.2 show a high degree of sectoral concentration of Indian ventures overseas, particularly in case of WOSs where more than one-half of the ventures are concentrated over trading and marketing of general nature and computer industry, mainly software. The former shares 35.12 per cent of the total number of ventures, while the latter claims 15.07 per cent of them. If one adds to it the financial and non-financial services and consultancy and management services, the percentage moves up to 65.86. All this means domination of the non-manufacturing activities. Among the manufacturing activities, the products which dominate are

Table 7.1 Geographic Pattern of India's Overseas Ventures
(as on 31 Dec. 1998)

| WOSs | | | | | | Non-WOSs | | | | | |
| Developed world | | | Developing world | | | Developed world | | | Developing world | | |
Country	No.	%	Country	No.	%	Country	No.	%	Country	No.	%
US	228	47.5	Singapore	100	29.2	US	91	32.4	UAE	66	10.5
UK	138	28.8	Mauritius	72	21.0	UK	83	29.5	Sri Lanka	64	10.2
Germany	24	5.0	Hong Kong	31	9.4	Russia	36	12.8	Malaysia	54	8.6
Russia	18	3.8	UAE	23	6.7	Germany	16	5.7	Singapore	53	8.6
Netherlands	18	3.8	Sri Lanka	13	3.7	Netherlands	11	3.9	Nepal	48	7.6
Switzerland	14	2.9				Australia	11	3.9	Thailand	29	4.5
Others	40	8.2	Others	104	30.0	Others	33	11.8	Others	315	50.0
Total	480	100	Total	343	100	Total	281	100	Total	629	100

Source: Indian Investment Centre documents.

textiles and garments, herbal and pharmaceutical products, chemicals, iron and steel products and food and beverages. They accounted collectively for 15.18 per cent of the total number of WOSs at the end of December 1998.

The case of non-WOSs is slightly different. The degree of concentration is not so high. Table 7.2 shows that trading and marketing activities on the top share only 16.37 per cent of the ventures. Adding to this the other non-manufacturing activities, such as financial and non-financial services, including consultancy and construction services, software, and travel and tourism along with hotels and restaurants, the percentage moves up to 44.5, much less than in case of the WOSs. Among the manufacturing activities, the products are almost the same as in the case of the WOSs. The collective share of chemicals, pharmaceuticals, food and beverages, textiles, and garment comes to 30 per cent.

The pattern of sectoral spread of Indian firms, whether through WOSs or through non-WOSs, clearly indicates that they have moved preferably to those areas where their basic objectives behind internationalization are achieved or where they have some sort of competitive advantage. One of the major objectives is to find a foreign market, either because technology imported from the industrialized world is meant for a market larger than the size of the Indian market, or because the conditions imposed by the Indian Government while permitting the import of technology make export mandatory. In order to fulfil the objectives, they have set up their trading and marketing office in different countries — developed and developing.

Indian firms have moved in a big way to provide financial and non-financial services. This is because they possess competitive advantage in a large trained manpower in the country. When, in a labour-surplus economy, the government provides technical and managerial education on a large scale, a big pool of trained manpower is created. It can be used easily by the domestic firms either for domestic or for foreign operation. In fact, Indian firms are enjoying a similar advantage.

The presence of Indian firms abroad in areas such as gems and jewellery, textiles and garments, leather goods, various

Table: 7.2 Sectoral Pattern of India's Overseas Ventures
(as on 31.12.1998)

	WOSs			Non–WOSs	
Sectors	No.	% Share	Sectors	No.	% share
Trading and marketing	289	35.12	Trading & marketing	149	16.37
Computers	124	15.07	Chemicals	80	8.79
Non-financial services	62	7.53	Pharmaceuticals and herbal products	71	7.80
Financial services	41	4.98	Consultancy	63	6.92
Textiles and garments	32	3.88	Food products and beverages	61	6.70
Consultancy and management	26	3.16	Textiles & garment	61	6.70
Pharmaceuticals and herbal products	26	3.16	Non-financial services	57	6.26
Chemicals	25	3.04	Computers	51	5.60
Iron and steel and its products	21	2.55	Financial services	43	4.73
Food products and beverages	21	2.55	Travel and tourism incl. Hotels and rest.	42	4.62
Total incl. others	823	100.00	Total incl. others	910	100.00

Source: Indian Investment Centre documents.

types of chemicals and pharmaceuticals is indicative of the fact that the they possess competitive advantage in labour-intensive modes of production. Indian firms in general have not achieved competitive advantage in capital-intensive modes of production compared to those in the industrialized countries and so they have preferably moved into areas involving labour-intensive modes of production.

There are cases, of course not many, where the Indian firms have gone abroad to exploit cheap raw material. We have already mentioned a few examples of Indian firms moving to Nepal for herbal preparations, to Bangladesh for the manufacture of paper and paper products and to Sri Lanka for the manufacture of rubber goods.

Sectoral Pattern across Countries

Three-fifths of the WOSs involved in trading activities are concentrated only in four countries, the US, Singapore, Mauritius and the UK (see Table A 7.1). Similarly, over two-thirds of the WOSs engaged in financial as well as non-financial services are concentrated in these countries. Again over 88 per cent of the WOSs engaged in information technology (computer software and hardware) are concentrated over only two countries, viz the US and Singapore. Indian firms in general find it difficult to compete with firms in these countries in the areas or sectors where sophisticated technology is involved. On the contrary, they find no resistance in trading and marketing and it is here that they can augment their export. As regards computer software, India has made considerable advances and Indian firms are able to penetrate into foreign markets. Indian firms have moved to the Middle East, Malaysia and Nigeria and a few other developing countries in the areas of consultancy services, project exports, management contracts, and also manufacture of iron and steel products since Indian firms possess technological superiority as compared to these countries.

About two-thirds of non-WOS joint ventures in food products exist only in five countries, viz. Nepal, Sri Lanka, UAE, Russia and the UK. This is partly because of the agrarian base of Indian firms and partly due to the demand for Indian food products by the large number of Indians in many of these countries.

Foreign-exchange Earnings due to Overseas Investment

It has already been mentioned that overseas ventures bring home dividend and other receipts and also give rise to additional exports. Now it would be worthwhile to see whether this argument holds good in the Indian context. However, such earnings cannot be compared with the foreign-exchange outflow on account of investment in the present study since there is always a time lag between the investment outflow and the generation of dividend and additional exports. Thus the present study shows the inflow of foreign-exchange earnings since 1993 rather than in 1992 which represents the pre-liberalization period in this context.

Table 7.3 shows that the total inflow at the end of 1992 stood at Rs 8.646 billion out of which dividend amounted to Rs 632.8 million, other remittances stood at Rs 1.030 billion and a sum of Rs 6.983 billion were the additional exports generated on this account. The share of non-WOSs in all these receipts was larger than those in the case of WOSs. Against this backdrop, we can see that such inflows went on increasing each successive year. On the basis of the available figures, there was an increase of over three-fold in foreign-exchange earnings during the period 1992–June 1998 — from Rs 8.646 billion at the end of 1992 to Rs 26.938 billion at the end of June 1998.

It is also evident from the figures that the share of dividend has always been the lowest. Other remittances have been roughly twice that of the dividend figure. The amount of exports generated formed the lion's share of such inflows ranging between 73 and 89 per cent of total such flows. The share of non-WOSs has always been larger than that of the WOSs mainly because their number has been larger in the total number of ventures operating abroad. Whatever the size of different segments of the inflow, the entire picture is very

Table 7.3   Foreign Exchange Earnings of India's Overseas Ventures

Amount in Rs million

	Values at the end of the period					
	1992	1993	1994	1995	1997	June 1998
A. Non-WOSs	5271.8	5974.1	9947.2	13974.3	n.a	16177.0
i. Dividend	482.6	622.4	778.3	834.7	n.a	1961.4
ii. Other repatriations	791.0	902.7	1137.7	1276.8	n.a	3011.6
iii. Additional exports generated	3998.2	4449.0	8031.2	11862.8	n.a	11204.0
B. WOSs	3374.3	5223.6	8485.1	9239.4	n.a	10760.7
i. Dividend	150.2	163.6	232.0	276.7	n.a	771.5
ii. Other repatriations	239.2	370.0	768.0	776.6	n.a	1973.0
iii. Additional exports generated	2984.9	4690.0	7485.1	8186.1	n.a	8016.2
C. Total (A+B)	8646.1	11197.7	18432.3	23213.7	25497.8	26937.7
i. Dividend	632.8	786.0	1010.3	1111.4	2183.2	2732.9
ii. Other repatriations	1030.2	1272.7	1905.7	2053.4	4844.6	4984.6
iii. Additional exports generated	6983.1	9139.0	15516.3	20048.9	18470.0	19220.2

Note: The figures for 1996 are not available.
Source: Government of India, *Ministry of Commerce Annual Report*, New Delhi, various issues.

bright from the view of the strengthening balance of payments.

Conclusion

In the process of economic reform, the Indian Government liberalized the policy concerning the country's overseas investment with the aim of improving the current account balance through greater repatriation of dividend, royalty, technical fees, etc., and by encouraging additional exports from ventures operating abroad. It was a feasible proposition in view of the fact that India possessed a strong technological base and, in many cases, its products had attained maturity in the international markets. The improved managerial skill was a plus point in this respect.

The liberalization package, consisting of smoothening procedural formalities and raising the investment ceiling, had a positive impact on investment in overseas ventures. There was tremendous growth in the number of approval of overseas ventures as well as in the amount of investment involved therein which surged. This was true in both the cases — WOSs and non-WOSs abroad. However, the WOSs were largely directed to the developed countries, whereas the non-WOSs moved mainly to the developing world. Again, a higher degree of geographic concentration was evident in case of WOSs than in non-WOSs.

The areas into which the firms moved were primarily services and trading and specific manufactures where the firms possessed competitive advantage. The competitive advantage was either on account of product and technology specifications or due to location. These products were primarily computer software, textiles and garments, food products, and herbals and pharmaceuticals.

Finally, in view of large approvals and operation of overseas ventures, the economy was able to earn a large amount of foreign exchange through various repatriations as well as generation of additional export.

Table A 7.1 Countrywise/sectorwise Distribution of WOSs Abroad

Region/country	1	2	3	4	5	6	7	8	9	10	11	12	13	14	15	16	17	18	19	20	21	Total
Africa																						
Botswana				1																		1
Ivory Coast			1																			1
Kenya			2												1				1			4
Mauritius	12	7	24	1	2		1	1	3		1	3	5	1	1						10	72
Mozambique										1												1
Namibia			1									2										3
Nigeria			1																			1
South Africa									1		1		1									3
Tanzania																		1			1	2
Uganda			2															1				3
Zambia			1													1						2
Zimbabwe				1																		1
Total	12	7	32	3	2		1	1	4	1	2	5	6	1	2	1		2	1		11	94
America																						
Bahamas			1	1																		2
Belize								1														1
Bermuda		2									1											3
Brazil			1																			1
Canada			1	1											1							3
Cayman Is.			1																			1

Table A 7.1 contd.

Region/country	1	2	3	4	5	6	7	8	9	10	11	12	13	14	15	16	17	18	19	20	21	Total
US	1	20	64	3					6		78	6	2	2		4	5	4			33	228
Total	1	22	68	5				1	6		79	6	2	2	1	4	5	4	2		33	239
East Asia																						
China		1	1		1													1				4
Hong Kong	3	1	13								2				3	2			2		5	31
Indonesia			1	2																		3
Japan											2								1			3
Malaysia	1	2	4	2		1						1										11
Singapore	3	12	34	1	2	1		2			22	1	3				3				16	100
South Korea																1						1
Thailand			1														1					2
Viet Nam									1													1
Total	7	16	54	5	3	2		2	1		26	2	3		3	3	4	1	3		21	156
Europe																						
Austria	2				2						1						2					7
Azerbaijan			1																			1
Belgium	1		5		2								1				1	1				11
British Virginia																				1	2	3
Bulgaria		1	1																1			3
Channel Is.	1	1	1																			3
Cyprus			6																		1	7

Table A 7.1 contd.

Table A 7.1 contd.

Region/country	1	2	3	4	5	6	7	8	9	10	11	12	13	14	15	16	17	18	19	20	21	Total
Czeck																					1	1
France		1	1																			2
Germany			13	3	2			1			1					1	2		1			24
Hungary				1																		1
Ireland			2	1											3							6
Jersey Channel												1				1						2
Kazkhastan			1																			1
Kirghistan			1																			1
Luxembourg	3													1								4
Netherlands			9									2	1		4		1	1				18
Poland			1														2					3
Russia	1		12												1			3			1	18
Sweden											1	1										2
Switzerland		1	11								1	1										14
Turkey									1													1
UK	16	10	49	8	1	2			1		10	11	9		6		3	2	2		8	138
Ukraine			2												1							3
Uzbekistan			2												1							3
Total	21	16	118	13	6	4			2		13	16	11	1	16	2	11	8	3		13	274
Oceania																						
Australia			1																1			2
New Zealand										1												1
Total			1							1									1			3

Table A 7.1 contd.

Table A 7.1 contd.

Region/country	1	2	3	4	5	6	7	8	9	10	11	12	13	14	15	16	17	18	19	20	21	Total
South Asia																						
Bangladesh	1		2								1			1								5
Maldives												2										2
Nepal			1		1						1		2		4		1		2			12
Sri Lanka			2		4			1			1	1	1					1	1		1	13
Total	1		5		5			1			3	3	3	1	4		1	1	3		1	32
West Asia																						
Bahrain					1														1			2
UAE			11		4	2			4							1					1	23
Total			11		5	2			4							1			1		1	25
Grand Total	41	62	289	26	21	8	1	5	17	1	124	32	25	5	26	11	21	16	12		80	823

Note: The figures relate to those operating and under implementation at the end of December 1995 and those approved during 1996, 1997 and 1998.

Source: Indian Investment Centre documents.

Sector/industry: 1. Financial services, 2. Non-financial services, 3. Trading and marketing, 4. Consultancy, management and construction, 5. Iron and steel and its products, 6. Machine and tool, instruments and engineering products, 7. Telecommunication, 8. Construction and building material including real estate, 9. Electrical goods and appliances including electronic appliances, 10. Automobiles, 11. Computers – hardware and software, 12. Textiles and garments, 13. Chemicals, 14. Paper and printing, 15. Pharmaceuticals and herbal products, 16. Gems and jewellery, 17. Food and beverages, 18. Leather, rubber and plastic products, 19. Hotels and restaurants including travel and tourism, 20. Glass and ceramics, 21. Others.

Table A 7.2 Countrywise/sectorwise Non-WOS Ventures Abroad

Region/country	1	2	3	4	5	6	7	8	9	10	11	12	13	14	15	16	17	18	19	20	21	Total
Africa																						
Botswana	1																					1
Egypt		1	1						2				2	2	1							9
Ghana															1							1
Guyana									1													1
Kenya	2		2						3	1		1	1	1			1	1				13
Liberia			1																			1
Mauritius	4	1	3	1		1		1	2		3	1	1	1	5			1		1		26
Morocco																					1	1
Nigeria			1	6	1			1	2			2	2		3		1					19
Senegal													3									3
Seychelles																			1			1
South Africa			1														2		1			4
Tanzania			2		1							3										6
Uganda			1						1			1			2							5
Zambia			1										1									2
Zimbabwe	1																					1
Total	8	2	13	7	2	1	1	2	11	1	3	8	10	4	12		4	2	2	1	1	94
Oceania																						
Australia		1	3								1		2	2					2			11
Fiji													1									1

Table A 7.2 contd.

Region/country	1	2	3	4	5	6	7	8	9	10	11	12	13	14	15	16	17	18	19	20	21	Total
Solomon Is.													1									1
Tonga													1									1
Vanuatu													1									1
Total		1	3								1		6	2					2			15
Europe																						
Austria															1							1
Azerbaijan												1			1							2
Belgium			1		1							1	1			1						5
Belorussia			1																			1
Bulgaria			1																			1
Channel Is.												2										2
Cyprus			1					1														2
Finland				1																	1	2
France			2														1					3
Georgia												1					1					2
Germany		2	7	2								3				1				1		16
Greece										2												2
Hungary			1									1	1		1			1	1			6
Ireland											1							1				2
Italy			2						1			1						1				5
Kazakhstan															3		1	3	2			9
Khirgystan													2	2								4

Table A 7.2 contd.

Region/country	1	2	3	4	5	6	7	8	9	10	11	12	13	14	15	16	17	18	19	20	21	Total
Latvia																	1					1
Leichenstein		1	1					1														3
Netherlands			2								1	3					1		4			11
Poland											1						1					2
Portugal									1													1
Russia			9	2		2		2	2		2	1	1		3		7	2	3			36
Slovak												1										1
Spain			1												1							2
Switzerland			4			1																5
Tadjikistan															3							3
Turkmenistan			1						1						2			1				5
UK	8	9	19			2		1	11	1	2	2	1		4		8	3	3		9	83
Ukraine											1								2			3
Uzbekistan			5						1		3	3			4		2					18
Yugoslavia					1																	1
Total	8	12	57	9	3	5		5	16	3	19	19	5	2	28	2	22	11	16	1	10	240
East Asia																						
China		2					1	1	1	1		1										7
Hong Kong		2	1		4			1	1	1		1	1		5	1			3			21
Indonesia			1		1	1			1	1	7	1	4	2		1	1					21
Japan		1	1						1			1				1	1					6
Malaysia	2	4	2	10	3	2			6		4	9	2	2	3		2	2	1			54

Table A 7.2 contd.

Table A 7.2 contd.

Region/country	1	2	3	4	5	6	7	8	9	10	11	12	13	14	15	16	17	18	19	20	21	Total
Mongolia												1										1
Philippines			1																			1
Singapore	3	10	12	9	2	3	1				4		3	2	1		2		1			53
South Korea				1							1											2
Thailand		2	2	3	2	3	1					4	4	2	4			2				29
Viet Nam									2												1	3
Total	5	17	26	25	12	9	3	1	9	4	7	16	23	6	14	2	6	4	7	1	1	198
South Asia																						
Bangladesh	3	2	2		1			1	1	1	3	1	3	1	1					1	1	22
Maldives																			2			2
Myanmar			1																		1	2
Nepal	3	2	2					4					6		6		12	4	7		2	48
Sri Lanka	5	4	3	1	5				2	3		7	7	2	2		7	4	3		9	64
Total	11	8	8	1	6			5	3	4	3	8	16	3	9		19	8	12	1	13	138
West Asia																						
Baharain	1		1	1	1						5			1			1				3	14
Iran	1	1											1									3
Israel												1	1									2
Jordon	1		1										2									4
Kuwait	1	1					1															3
Oman		2		4									3				1					10
Saudi Arabia		3		4				1					2					1	1		1	13
UAE	3	3	13	6	12			1	3	2	2	2			2		6	4	1	1	5	66

Table A 7.2 contd.

Table A 7.2 contd.

Region/country	1	2	3	4	5	6	7	8	9	10	11	12	13	14	15	16	17	18	19	20	21	Total
Total	6	10	15	15	13		2	2			7	3	13	1	2	1	8	5	2	1	9	115
America																						
Bahamas				1							1											2
Brazil				1																		1
Canada			2				1								1							4
Cayman Is.												1										1
Jersey Channel Is												1										1
Mexico			2																			2
Panama	1	2						2	1			1										7
US	3	5	23	4	1	1	1	1	1		23	4	7	1	5		2		1		8	91
Trinidad & Tobago	1																					1
Total	5	7	27	6	1	1	2	3	2		24	7	7	1	6		2		1		8	110
Grand Total	43	57	149	63	37	16	7	18	41	12	51	61	80	19	71	5	61	30	42	5	42	910

Notes: The figures relate to those in operation and under implementation at the end of Dec. 1995 and those approved in 1996, 1997 and 1998.

Source: Indian Investment Centre documents.

Sector/industry: 1. Financial services, 2. Non-financial services, 3. Trading and marketing, 4. Consultancy, management and construction, 5. Iron and steel and its products, 6. Machine and tool, instruments and engineering products, 7. Telecommunication, 8. Construction and building material including real estate, 9. Electrical goods and appliances including electronic appliances, 10. Automobiles, 11. Computers – hardware and software, 12. Textiles and garments, 13. Chemicals, 14. Paper and printing, 15. Pharmaceuticals and herbal products, 16. Gems and jewellery, 17. Food

8

External Indebtedness

Due to the heavy external indebtedness in the early 1990s, the thrust of the external sector reform in India has been mainly on reducing the debt burden. The Indian government not only emphasized the foreign-investment channel that could substitute foreign borrowings but also redesigned the policy concerning foreign borrowing. This chapter discusses the nature of the policy and evaluates its impact on arresting the growth in the quantum of external debt. We begin with the concept of indebtedness and the factors that led to this phenomenal growth in India's external indebtedness during the late 1980s and early 1990s.

Concept of External Debt

External assistance and foreign borrowings help bridge the investment-savings gap as well as the import-export gap and thereby permit the warranted rate of investment and the desired rate of growth. Dragoslav Avramovic (1964) posits an optimal path of growth with foreign borrowings according to which the process of development is divided into three phases. The first is characterized by a heavy inflow of foreign borrowings to meet the required investment as well as to make service payments on foreign loans. The magnitude of external indebtedness keeps growing very fast. In the second phase, domestic savings as well as export earnings grow in the same magnitude as investment. The country still borrows to service the debt. Indebtedness in this phase rises but not as fast as in the first phase. In the third phase, domestic resources grow such that they meet the current investment needs but also service past loans. Indebtedness begins to lessen and after some time it disappears. The process of growth becomes self-sustaining. However, constraints to this optimal path may arise if:

- the availability of foreign loans is not sufficient enough to push up the desired rate of investment and to service past loans
- the types of loans are not very conducive to the process of development
- the terms of the borrowed funds are hard enough to cause greater indebtedness
- the borrowed funds are not utilised properly to help generate desired output in the borrowing country

Goran Ohlin (1966) discusses the impact of varying terms of loans on the inflow-outflow pattern. The higher the interest rate, the lower is the net availability of loans for development purposes. For example if a country receives a loan each year for $ 1,000 repayable in 12 equal annual instalments, including a grace period of two years, different interest rates will have varying impact on the inflow-outflow pattern. At 5 per cent interest rate, service charges will rise so fast that only after nine years, the country will actually be paying out more by way of interest and amortization than it is receiving in the form of new loans. At 3 per cent interest rate, the net outflow will occur only from the eleventh year onward. At 1 per cent interest rate, the net outflow will begin from the twelfth year.

Similarly, the impact is different for varying periods of repayment. Purely in a mathematical framework, it is found that a longer repayment period and a longer grace period increase the amount of servicing as interest is paid over a longer period. However, when one takes into account the time required for the generation of domestic savings, longer grace and repayment periods are preferred. This is because the borrowing country gets time to generate resources for the purpose of servicing foreign loans. Which of the two is preferable depends on the nature of returns. Short-term loans are advisable where quick and high pay-off is expected. In other cases, long-term loans are advisable.

Besides the terms, the types of loans are also important. For example, bilateral loans are normally tied to purchases in the donor country. In such cases, the price of supplies under the loan agreement is usually inflated and this lowers the contribution of loans (Bhagwati, 1970). From this point of view, multilateral loans are preferable. If there is under-utilized industrial capacity in the borrowing countries, it may be advisable to have non-project loans that could finance the import of raw material, spares, and other input.

The inflow of loans should be continual and in desired magnitude for the development process to be continuous, and in order to generate income and savings in the economy. Any interruption in the flow of loans will make the process of development discontinuous and will have an adverse impact on the capacity to repay. In fact, discontinuity in the flow of loan was one of the reasons behind unmanageable indebtedness among a large number of developing countries during early 1980s.

Finally, the amount of borrowed funds should be utilized in an efficacious manner in order to generate sufficient output. Unfortunately, in a large number of countries, one finds several instances of the administrative machinery too weak to allow proper utilization of the borrowed funds (Reilly, 1987; Sharan, 1991), resulting in heavy borrowing to service past loans. This increases the debt burden further impinging on the very process of development.

India's External Debt Burden during the Early 1990s

Foreign loans have played a significant role in bridging the resource gap in India's economic development (Sharan, 1975). External indebtedness did increase over the decades, but intensified in pace after the first half of the 1980s. In fact, this was the result of unwarranted movement of some macroeconomic variables more significant of which was a large fiscal deficit during 1980s. The high level of fiscal deficit was partly covered by domestic borrowings. The issue of treasury bills led to growing monetization of debt resulting in the double-digit inflation level. The government raised the statutory liquidity ratio of commercial banks in order to mop up resources, but that affected the profitability of the banks and the very health of the monetary and financial sectors of the economy. In such circumstances, the government resorted to large-scale borrowing from abroad for the purpose of covering the fiscal deficit thus causing greater indebtedness.

Huge fiscal deficit alone was not the sole cause for external indebtedness. It was the growing size of current account deficit after the second oil shock that forced the government into external borrowing. Chapter 2 described how the growth rate of exports lagged behind imports and the factors responsible for this. It is also evident how the net earnings on the invisibles account showed a sluggish trend. This period showed a growing current account deficit. FDI inflow had grown and covered a small part of the deficit on the current account, but in view of the economic and political instability during the late 1980s and early 1990s, it seemed a bit sluggish during this period and failed to entirely substitute the foreign borrowings.

The problem with foreign borrowings would not have been as grave with inflow of concessional loans. Jalan (1991) finds that in case of multilateral loans also, the share of non-concessional loans increased during the 1980s but that too was not sufficiently available. In the absence of desired availability of concessional and non-concessional assistance from government sources, there was an increase in commercial borrowing. Since commercial borrowings carried very high rate of interest as well as shorter maturity, they greatly added to external indebtedness. Harder-term loans led to bigger servicing payments which in turn reduced the net availability of loans and the productivity of the foreign borrowings. A vicious circle of external indebtedness was very much apparent during the early 1990s. Statistics (GOI, 1993; GOI, 1994) show that India's external indebtedness was increasing. The magnitude of external debt moved up from $ 23.5 billion in 1980–1 to $ 83.96 by March 1991 and to $ 85.33 by March 1992. Its share in GDP went up from 13.7 per cent to 30.7 per cent and to 41.1 per cent during the corresponding period. The growth in service payments did not lag behind. It was from $ 1.41 billion to $ 8.13 billion and to $ 8.22 billion during the above period that accounted for 9.3 per cent, 31.9 per cent and 31.2 per cent respectively of the current account earnings. The comparison may not be very accurate in view of changed external debt format in the 1990s, but is approximately valid. The debt was definitely impeding the processes of economic development. Thus, the management of external debt was an important agendum for the macroeconomic reforms in the country.

Measures of Policy Reform to Cure External Indebtedness

Policy announcements were made so as to keep the Indian economic environment congenial for foreign investors — direct and portfolio — so that foreign investment inflow could substitute foreign borrowing. The Rangarajan Committee, constituted for balance of payments reform, made certain suggestions. First, commercial borrowings for less than five years of maturity were not to be encouraged. Second, NRI deposits for more than one-year maturity were to be encouraged to meet the medium-term financial needs. Third, short-term borrowings were to be made only for trade-related purposes. In fact, this was meant to shorten the size of service payments.

However, in the face of the changing external debt environment, there were some policy changes with respect to external commercial borrowings during 1997–8 and April–December 1998. It is very difficult to examine their impact at the present juncture and with the figures available to us. First, RBI can sanction such borrowings up to $ 10 million with a minimum average maturity of three years for specific purposes. This is in addition to the scheme under which the RBI considers the application from companies for raising such funds up to $ 5 million. Second, companies having foreign-exchange earnings are allowed to borrow up to three times of the average of annual export earnings during the previous three years, subject to a ceiling of $ 100 million. There is no end-use restriction except for investment in real estate or stock market. The proceeds can now be deployed for project-related rupee expenditure in all sectors subject to specific conditions. Third, holding companies are allowed to raise such loans up to $ 50 million to finance equity investment in a subsidiary company. Fourth, external commercial borrowings of eight-year maturity can be made up to $ 100 million and those of 16-year maturity can be made up to $ 200 million. Fifth, the cooling-off period for making fresh application for ECB (External Commercial Borrowings) stands reduced to one month. Finally, pre-payment facility is permitted if this is met out of inflow on account of foreign equity.

Impact of the Reforms

Structure of External Debt

We now examine whether the growth in external indebted-ness has decelerated during the period of reform. Table 8.1 shows that the total external indebtedness increased from $ 85.3 billion at the end of March 1992 to $ 99.0 billion at the end of March 1995 but decelerated to $ 93.5 billion by March 1997. Again, there was a rise in the quantum of external debt, $ 93.9 billion by March 1998 and $ 98.2 billion by March 1999. Thus the favourable trend in form of decreasing debt burden, which was evident after 1994–5, could not last long. That the burden has started increasing again since 1998–9 raises a question mark on the efficacy of reform measures.

On anatomizing further the structure of external debt, it is revealed that the share of official debt moved up from 60.3 per cent at the end of March 1991 to 63.5 per cent by March 1994, but began to shrink marginally thereafter and by the end of September 1997, it was 58.1 per cent (GOI, 1998). Similarly, the share of short-term debt, which had witnessed a squeeze in the initial years of reform—from 8.3 per cent of total debt at the end of March 1992 to barely 3.9 per cent at the end of March 1994—tended to increase till March 1997 when it was of the order of 7.3 per cent. However, this percentage fell to

Amount in $ billions

Forms of debt	At the end of March							
	1992	1993	1994	1995	1996	1997	1998	1999
Multilateral: out of which	23.1	25.0	26.3	28.5	28.6	29.2	29.6	30.6
concessional	14.3	15.5	16.0	17.8	17.6	17.6	17.8	18.6
Non-concessional	8.8	9.5	10.3	10.7	11.0	11.6	11.8	12.0
Bilateral: out of which	15.5	16.2	17.5	20.3	19.0	17.4	17.1	17.5
concessional	13.5	14.0	15.0	17.4	16.1	14.3	13.2	13.9
Non-concessional	2.0	2.2	2.5	2.9	2.9	3.0	3.9	3.6
IMF borrowings	3.5	4.8	5.0	4.3	2.4	1.3	0.7	0.3
Export credit	4.0	4.3	5.2	6.6	5.4	5.9	6.7	6.7
Commercial loans	11.7	11.6	12.4	13.0	13.9	14.3	17.0	21.8
NRIs' deposits	10.1	11.1	12.7	12.4	11.0	11.0	12.0	12.3
Rupee debt	10.4	10.6	10.1	9.6	8.2	7.5	5.9	4.7
Total long-term debt	78.2	83.7	89.1	94.7	88.7	86.7	88.9	93.9
Short-term debt	7.1	6.3	3.6	4.3	5.0	6.7	5.0	4.3
Total debt	85.3	90.0	92.7	99.0	93.7	93.5	93.9	98.2
Concessional as percentage of total	44.8	44.5	44.4	45.3	45.5	42.8	33.0	37.9
Short-term as percentage of total	8.3	7.0	3.9	4.3	5.5	7.3	5.3	4.4

Sources: Government of India, (1999) *Economic Survey 1998–9*, New Delhi: Ministry of Finance, pp. S-110-11. Government of India, (1999) *India's External Debt: A Status Report* New Delhi; Ministry of Finance, pp. 1-8. Reserve Bank of India, (1999) *Annual Report 1998–9*, Bombay, pp. 230-31.

4.4 by March 1999. Since short-term debt tends to inflate the servicing burden, the confinement of its share in the total debt within a limited range is always beneficial.

The share of debt related to concessional assistance — multilateral, bilateral and rupee assistance — has been confined to well around one-half of the total debt. However, the share of commercial debt increased especially after 1995-6 and reached 22.2 per cent at the end of March 1999 compared to 14.8 per cent at the end of March 1996. This trend is not favourable in the sense that the servicing burden will be larger on account of higher interest rate commercial borrowings.

Borrower Classification

The borrower classification of external debt indicates that the share of government in total external debt that was hovering around 60 per cent between March 1991 and March 1995, dropped to around 51 per cent by September 1998. This was due to the decline in rupee-denominated debt and the IMF debt during this period.

Trends in Debt Service

After the analysing of the structure of external debt, we now analyse the burden of servicing the external debt. Table 8.3 shows that India's debt-service payments increased from $ 8.99 billion in 1990-1 to $ 12.3 billion during 1996-7. But then it decreased to $ 11.4 billion during 1997-8 and to $ 10.7 billion during 1998-9. The amount of repayments was always larger than the amount of interest payments. Moreover, the share of repayments in total debt service payments increased from 55.97 per cent in 1990-1 to 60.51 per cent in 1997-8.

The drop in the debt-service payments after 1996-7 is mainly because of a reduction in such payments in respect of external commercial borrowings and external assistance as well as in respect of borrowings from the IMF. Those concerning rupee debt and NRI deposits tended to inflate. Nevertheless, during 1998-9, the largest segment of debt service payments being 43.31 per cent was represented by external commercial borrowings, followed by 29.30 per cent

Table 8.2   India's External Debt: Government and Non-government Components

$ million

	End-March							End-Sept
	1991	1992	1993	1994	1995	1996	1997P	1998P
Government account	33.75	36.74	38.96	40.86	45.29	43.36	41.59	41.29
Defence	13.59	10.84	10.87	10.04	9.91	7.36	6.16	5.41
IMF	2.62	3.45	4.80	5.04	4.30	2.37	1.31	0.95
Government debt	49.96	51.03	54.63	55.94	59.50	53.09	49.06	47.65
Non-government debt	33.84	34.26	35.39	36.76	39.51	39.11	43.16	45.23
Total	83.80	85.29	90.02	92.70	99.01	92.20	92.22	92.88
Government debt as a proportion of total debt	59.6	59.8	60.7	60.4	60.1	57.6	53.2	51.3

Note: The definition of government debt here includes debt on government account maintained by the Controller of Aid Accounts and Audit, IMF and defence.
All others including short tern debt are part of non- Government debt. Defence and PSU debt figures are included as part of non- Government debt from 1996 onwards.
Source: Government of India, (1998) *Status Report*, New Delhi: Ministry of Finance.

by those on external assistance and 16.02 per cent by those on NRI deposits. The rest pertained to the borrowings from the IMF and to the rupee debt.

However, the redeeming feature is that the debt-GDP ratio that was as high as 41 per cent in 1990–1 and 39.8 per cent during 1992–3 began descending in the following years and came down to a figure as low as 23.8 per cent during 1997–8. This was not all. The debt-service ratio too fell significantly during the period of reform — from 30.2 per cent during 1990–1 to 19.8 per cent during 1997–8 and to 18.0 per cent in 1998–9. Debt-current receipt ratio too fell from a level of 323.4 per cent in 1992–3 to 161.1 per cent in 1997–8, although slightly ascending to 164.4 per cent in the following financial year. The improvement in the debt-service indicators is really a positive aspect of the economic reforms.

International Comparison

The impact of economic reform on the country's external indebtedness is clearer against the background of the international scenario. According to the World Bank figures, India has been among the top ten developing country debtors. India ranked third after Brazil and Mexico in 1993 but by 1996 its indebtedness improved considerably as it was ranked after seven developing countries (the first six being Brazil, Mexico, Indonesia, China, the Russian Federation, Argentina and Thailand). This is definitely the bright aspect of the economic reforms.

However, the debt-service payments, as presented in Table 8.4, are still very high and that is a matter of concern. India holds the fifth position for the debt-service ratio among 10 top indebted countries. As regards the debt-GNP ratio India is the seventh.

Present Value of External Debt

Debt disbursed and outstanding is not a good measure for making international comparisons, since the composition of debt concessionality varies considerably. To obtain appropriate weightage for concessionality of debt, we need to evaluate the

Table 8.3   India's External Debt Service Payments

$ million

	1991–2	1992–3	1993–4	1994–5	1995–6	1996–7	1997–8	1998–9
1. External assistance	2447	2541	2968	3186	3691	3283	3229	3144
repayments	1329	1443	1645	1748	2192	1922	1966	
interest	1118	1098	1323	1438	1499	1361	1263	
2. External commercial borrowing	2830	2707	3232	4290	4578	5626	4934	4648
repayments	1677	1525	1978	2812	3176	4303	3550	
interest	1153	1182	1254	1478	1402	1323	1384	
3. IMF	697	614	387	1368	1860	1061	667	419
repayments	459	335	134	1146	1715	975	618	
interest	238	279	253	222	145	86	49	
4. Non-resident Indian deposits interest	1036	918	905	1046	1247	1627	1807	1719
5. Rupee debt service	1240	878	1053	983	952	727	767	802
6. Total debt service	8250	7658	8545	10732	12328	12324	11404	10732
repayments	4705	4181	4810	6689	8035	7927	6901	
interest	3545	3477	3735	4043	4293	4397	4503	
7. Current receipts	27307	27839	33629	41988	49636	55240	57538	59760
8. Debt-current receipt ratio per cent	312.4	323.4	275.6	235.8	188.9	169.6	161.1	164.4

Table 8.3 contd.

Table 8.3 contd.

$ million

	1991–2	1992–3	1993–4	1994–5	1995–6	1996–7	1997–8	1998–9
9. Debt-GDP ratio per cent	41.0	39.8	35.8	32.3	28.2	25.9	23.8	
10. Debt service ratio per cent	30.2	27.5	25.3	25.6	24.8	22.2	19.8	18.0

* Inclusive of non-government account figures supplied by the office of Controller of Aid Accounts and Audit, Ministry of Finance.
# Excludes accrued interest on India Development Bonds (IDBs). For 1996–7, only that component of principal repayment on IDBs is taken as debt service which is redeemed in foreign exchange.
Sources: Government of India, (1999) *Economic Survey 1998–9*, New Delhi: Ministry of Finance, pp. S-110–11. Government of India, (1999) *India's External Debt: A Status Report* New Delhi; Ministry of Finance, pp. 1–8. Reserve Bank of India, (1999) *Annual Report 1998–9*, Bombay, pp. 230–31.

Table 8.4   External Debt Indicators of Highly Indebted Countries

Ranking country	Debt-GNP ratio %	Debt service ratio %
Brazil	24.5	41.1
Mexico	48.9	35.4
Indonesia	59.7	36.8
China	16.0	8.7
Russian federation	28.9	6.6
Argentina	32.3	44.2
Thailand	50.3	11.5
India	25.6	24.1
Turkey	43.4	21.7
Philippines	47.3	13.7

Source: The World Bank, (1998) *Global Development Finance, Volume II,* Washington D.C.

present value (PV) of debt which is arrived at by discounting the future stream of debt-service payments for individual loans by an appropriate discount rate and aggregating the PVs for all such loans. A country is classified as severely indebted if the ratio of external debt PV to current receipt is 220 per cent or more; moderately indebted if the ratio is between 132 and 220 per cent; and less indebted if it is less than 132 per cent (World Bank, 1998). The statistics show that PV of external debt-current receipts ratio for India was 214 per cent in 1994 – almost at the threshold level of severely indebted countries.

Conclusion

India's external debt burden reduced during the later years of economic reform, although it increased in 1998–9. Though there is improvement in the debt-service indicators, India still continues to be among the top ten indebted countries. Hence we need to pursue a more rational debt-management policy, prioritizing the use of commercial credit and encouraging foreign investment. Despite the fact that the short-term debt is well within limits, caution needs to be exercised to see that it is kept low.

9

An Overview

Pre-reform Scenario

It has been observed that during the pre-reform period, India's external sector was under continuous strain. The capital-account inflows on official account during this period fell far short of requirements. Net inflow on the private-capital account was modest and could only partially meet the current account deficit. As a consequence, large drawings were made from the IMF.

The current account of the country's balance of payments was adversely affected by three oil shocks since the early 1970s. Large import of food grains and fertilizers added to the problem. The Indian government's inward-looking strategy of industrialization was responsible for the rise in import of capital goods and components. The increased imports would not have posed any problem had exports kept pace with the increasing imports. Even though a number of incentives were provided to boost exports, the policy structure till the 1970s was primarily an inward-oriented one. The domestic market that was protected behind high tariff, continued to be more profitable than the export market. Since 1985 modest attempts were made in favour of a more outward-looking strategy. But the immediate impact of import liberalization was manifested in growing imports.

Turning to the capital account, it is evident that till the 1970s, even though the magnitude of external debt continued to increase and put pressure through the payments of principal, the net aid available was almost sufficient to meet the current account deficit. However, during the 1980s, availability of official aid fell short of meeting such deficit. Consequently, the government was compelled to go for commercial borrowings. The growing fiscal deficit was another factor behind the increasing inflow of commercial borrowings. The tougher terms lessened the net fund availability and pushed up external debt, forcing the government to approach the IMF. The external debt including the IMF borrowing turned so huge during the late 1980s that the debt/export ratio became comparable to that in other 17 heavily indebted countries of Asia, Africa, and Latin America.

The role that FDI played in meeting the balance of payment deficit is suspect. Some studies have demonstrated that imports necessitated by foreign-controlled rupee companies often exceeded the value of export generated by them. Also noticed was the uncertainty attached to private-capital flows. When the balance of payments crisis was the severest during the early 1990s, there was large-scale disinvestment by NRIs. The flow of FDIs dropped perceptibly. Thus the overall picture of India's external sector was not a comfortable one during the pre-reform period. It was this precarious position of the country's external account in the early 1990s that induced the launch of economic reform in this sector.

The Policy Package

Reforming of foreign trade was the first step in the process of India's external sector reform. The redesigning of foreign-trade sector policy was directed to four main areas: (i) rationalization of the exchange-rate policy, (ii) liberalization of import, (iii) provision of export incentives, and (iv) the simplification of procedural formalities and greater transparency.

In the very first week of July 1991, the rupee was depreciated so as to align the nominal exchange rate with the real exchange rate. Initially, a dual exchange-rate policy was introduced in March 1992; but within a year, full convertibility at uniform market-determined rate was introduced. By August 1994, the entire current-account earnings became convertible at market rates.

The reform measures sought to arrest trade deficit not through import compression, but through export expansion for which import liberalization was an essential pre-requisite. Under LERMS, capital goods and intermediates were freely importable subject to the payment of normal tariff. Beginning from 1992–3, the peak tariff rates were brought down significantly and import of capital goods was permitted at more favourable rates in order to improve the competitiveness of exports.

Quantitative restrictions have also been removed from the import of many items, particularly capital goods and intermediates. This has reduced the negative list of imports even though it still remains considerable. On the other hand, the open general-license list has been broadened. Many imports canalised through public sector agencies have been decanalised. The provisions of advance licence have been simplified. Further, a number of products have been transferred from the restricted list to the list of special import license.

The reform measures have strengthened the channels of export. EPZs, EOUs, export houses, trading houses, and star trading houses have been offered added incentives. The size of negative list of exports has been pruned. The cost and availability of export credit has been made more favourable. Besides, exporters have been permitted to retain up to 50 per cent of their export receipts in a designated account so as to reduce the conversion cost for their essential imports.

The reform measures have simplified procedures considerably. The trade and customs classification has been harmonized and the number of duty rates has been reduced. Besides, importers are automatically issued advance licenses on the basis of information furnished by them.

The economic reform measures directed towards FDI in the country have considerably diluted the provisions of FERA by enhancing the ceiling for foreign-equity participation and also by opening many areas of the economy for foreign investment.

The new policy has reduced the procedural formalities to a great extent and fostered transparency in this area.

The Indian government is relying greatly on NRIs for greater inflow of foreign investment into this country. To this end, they have been provided some additional incentives. In many areas, they are permitted to own the whole of the equity capital of Indian companies. They have been encouraged to make portfolio investments in the country. The RIBs were floated in August 1998 in order to mop up their savings and specific bank-deposit schemes have been drawn out for them.

In 1992 the Indian government allowed FPI to flow in. Indian companies were allowed to raise capital from abroad through the issue of Euro-equities and foreign-currency convertible bonds. FIIs were allowed to operate at the country's stock exchanges. In this process, the norms for Euro-issues have been liberalized considerably in order to boost such flows. The extent of investment by the FIIs has been raised as also foreign brokers are allowed to operate in the Indian capital market, although the SEBI keeps an eye on the transactions of the FIIs and foreign brokers.

Another component in the process of India's economic reform has been the liberalization of the country's overseas investment. The objective has been to improve the current account balance through greater repatriation of dividend, royalty, technical fees, etc. and through encouraging additional exports by the ventures operating abroad. The liberalization package involves the smoothening of procedural formalities and also the raising of the investment limit. Automatic approval is provided under certain conditions and the foreign-exchange balancing requirements have now been waived.

Finally, the policy package under the aegis of economic reform aims at reducing the burden of external indebtedness. This is why it attaches greater importance to foreign-investment inflow, both direct and portfolio, rather than to external borrowings. Various guidelines were issued in the beginning to curb the inflow of commercial borrowings, although, when the external-debt indicators began improving, the external commercial borrowing norms were eased. The short-term perspectives as well as the medium and long-term views are taken into account.

Impact of the Reforms

The impact of the economic reform policy package has been broadly positive, although there are some areas where desired results have yet to be achieved. Let us begin with the foreign-trade sector. The liberalization of exchange-rate regime and the adoption of the managed floating system has led to a continual fall in the value of the rupee — from Rs 31.36/$ in 1993–4 to Rs 42.39/$ in March 1999. What is surprising is that the depreciation in the value of currency has not been able to raise the export earning as is normally expected. The trade sector has marked oscillations in export earnings as well as in the import bill during the period of reform. In the recent past, imports have tended to stabilize, but the growth rate of export has been meagre with the result that the size of trade deficit has swollen even more in the recent years than what was witnessed during the pre-reform period. The external factors, beyond the control of the Indian government, have been largely responsible for arresting export performance, but the constraint on the infrastructural front and the prevalence of some other supply constraints cannot be denied. The reform measures in future must focus greatly on doing away with the supply constraints if the export growth scenario has to be improved.

The positive feature is that the export market has diversified and commodity concentration has reduced. More specifically, the terms of trade have improved conferring upon the country ample gains from trade.

The positive impact is more evident in the case of foreign investment. The amount of approved direct investment has increased phenomenally during the period of reform, except for a marginal sluggishness during 1998. The ratio of actual inflow has, however, remained confined within a lower limit either on account of procedural formalities or owing to lack of desired infrastructural support. The upsurge in this ratio in 1998 and in the first half of 1999 is nevertheless redeeming.

It is also a fact that FDI has flowed from different corners of the globe. Yet a sizeable segment of the approved amount or the actual flow is accounted for only by six or seven countries. The sectoral pattern has, however, come to be greatly broad-based covering not only the traditional sectors but also the non-traditional sectors. This is the positive impact of the opening up of new areas for foreign investors.

Yet again, the liberalization of the provisions for foreign-equity participation has resulted in coming up of a large number of wholly-owned subsidiaries and other subsidiaries with great stake in equity. Nevertheless, India is positioned on a lower rung among the major FDI recipients of Asia. The reforms have yet to go a long way in attracting large FDI inflows.

The role of NRIs has been significant. The amount of direct investment rose fast, although a downtrend emerged since 1997–8. The amount of the NRI portfolio investment has been small, except for 1998–9 when the RIBs helped mop up their savings considerably. In the initial years of reform, they showed interest in non-banking company deposits, but there has been a net withdrawal in the recent past. Their deposits with banks too have not shown an encouraging trend.

As far as portfolio investment in general is concerned, the response of the foreign investors was very good in the initial years. The amount of such inflows rose considerably. But since 1997–8, there is a marked downtrend. The flow of funds on account of Euro-issues has been meagre. During 1998–9, there was net disinvestment by the FIIs. Yet, on the whole, the contribution of FPI to the country's balance of payments has been sizeable though this has been marked by wide yearly fluctuations.

The liberal policy during the period of reform led to approval of a larger number of the country's ventures to operate abroad. The number of ventures going international or the amount of investment involved therein has been far larger than in the pre-reform period. Yet the country's overseas investment is much lower than that of some major foreign investing developing countries of Asia. More encouragement needs to be provided to the Indian firms moving abroad.

Ventures have moved to both the developed and the developing countries. However, the WOSs are highly concentrated over a few countries. The directional pattern of the non-WOS ventures is not so concentrated. The areas into which the firms have moved are primarily services and trading and those manufactures where the firms possess some kind of advantage, either on account of product and technology specifications or on account of location and mode of production, such as computer software, textiles and garments, food products, herbals and pharmaceuticals, and gems and jewellery.

Indian overseas ventures have been able to earn a significant value of foreign exchange through repatriations of various kinds and through generation of additional export, despite the fact that there exists a time lag between approvals and the inflow of foreign-exchange earnings.

In order to bridge the savings-investment gap as also to meet the current account deficit, India had to take recourse to foreign borrowings. The decline in the availability of official development assistance has meant increased private commercial borrowings. While it is true that India's external-debt position improved in some of the years of reform not only in absolute terms but also in comparison to other highly indebted countries, India continues to be a moderately indebted country according to World Bank classification and ranks among the top ten highly indebted developing countries (World Bank, 1999). Hence India needs to pursue a more rational debt-management policy, prioritizing the use of commercial credit and encouraging foreign investment. Further, even though India's short-term debt has been limited, caution needs to be exercised to see that the same is kept low and the mix of commercial borrowings is also kept within manageable limits.

The overall impact of economic reform in the country's external sector can be found in the recent trends in the balance of payments position. Table 9.1 presents an overview of the balance of payments during the period of reform as compared to the pre-reform period, 1990–1. It shows that the deficit on trade account, though relatively small in the first three fiscal years of reform, has gone on inflating and has come to be larger than that during 1990–1. There is improvement in the net earnings on invisibles account with the result that the deficit on the current account has been lower than the deficit on the trade account. Yet the current account deficit is large despite being lower than that in 1990–1.

The actual inflow of foreign investment has been far larger than in the pre-reform period, but the recent drop, especially in 1998–9 is not a positive feature. It is not worrisome if this is only a temporary phase.

The amount of loan, net of repayments, has begun moving upward again since 1996–7 after a decline during the immediately preceding years. In 1998–9, there has been a little check, and if this continues, external indebtedness should remain under manageable limits.

The overall balance of payments has normally been positive, except for two fiscal years, during the period of reform. This has resulted in an increase in the foreign-exchange reserves in almost all fiscal years of the reform era. The foreign-exchange reserves stood at over $ 32 billion at the end of March 1999 (RBI, 1999) compared to around $ 5 billion during 1990–1. The country's external sector has gained strength with economic reforms.

Conclusion

It is quite evident that the gains from external sector reform have been large. There has been increase in the approved amount of FDI in general and of the NRIs investment in particular, in the portfolio investment inflow and in the approval of the country's overseas investment. On the other hand, there has been a temporary lull in the recent past in the growth of exports leading to large current account deficits. The external-debt burden has been on the rise. India ranks low as the recipient of foreign investment as well as the provider of foreign investment compared to some other Asian developing countries. This requires the process of reforms to be deepened and enhanced. A period of about eight years is not sufficient for a complete metamorphosis of the external-sector. It needs more time particularly when the external-

Table 9.1   An Overview of India's Balance of Payments Position

Amount in $ million

	Pre-reform period	Period of reform							
	1990–1	1991–2	1992–3	1993–4	1994–5	1995–6	1996–7	1997–8	1998–9
Balance of trade	-9438	-2798	-5447	-4056	-9049	-11359	-14815	-15507	-13246
Invisibles	-242	1620	1921	2898	5680	5449	10196	10007	9208
Balance of current account	-9680	-1178	-3526	-1158	-3369	-5910	-4619	-5500	-4038
Foreign investment	103	133	557	4235	4807	4615	5963	5353	2312
External loans	5533	3979	411	1812	3035	2201	4795	4799	4418
Banking capital	682	564	3826	2263	-334	762	2229	-893	1480
Rupee debt	-1193	-1240	-878	-1053	-983	-952	-727	-767	-802
Other capital account flows	1931	474	-40	1638	1977	-2537	-254	1352	1157
Total capital account	7056	3910	3876	8895	8502	4089	12006	9844	8565
Overall balance incl. errors and omissions	-2492	2599	-590	8537	5787	- 1221	6793	4511	4222
Monetary movements:									
a. IMF	1214	786	1288	187	-1143	-1715	-975	-618	-393
b. Foreign exchange reserves: increase(–)/ decrease (+)	1278	-3385	-698	-8724	-4644	2936	-5818	-3893	-3829

Sources: 1. For the figures for 1991–2 to 1994–5, Government of India, (1999) *Economic Survey: 1998–9* New Delhi: Ministry of Finance.
2. Remaining figures from, *Reserve Bank of India Bulletin* (1999), Bombay Sept.

sector policy was not very liberal during about four decades preceding the present economic reform. As Jagdish Bhagwati (1998) felt, 'To some extent, changing India's uniquely damaging policy framework, nourished for over three decades, is a task akin to cleaning up after a typhoon: the task is enormous and cannot be done all at once.'

If external-sector reforms have to be fully successful, the process needs the backing of strong political will which is of utmost importance in a democratic set-up of the Indian economy. It has been witnessed that the coalition governments following the Narsimha Rao government were dependent upon the support of the left parties that were not in favour of liberalization. However, the Vajpayee government has been pro-reform and pro-liberalization despite being a coalition government. In the Budget speech of February 1999, the Indian Finance Minister reiterated his commitment for economic reform and announced fresh incentives and reform measures exclusively in the external sector. The Commerce Minister, too, stressed on the need for reducing the cost of export. In the recent months, some additional measures have been taken to strengthen the external sector. Presently, the National Democratic Alliance under Prime Minister Vajpayee's umbrella enjoys a comfortable majority in the Parliament that is an indication of continuance of strong political will in favour of reform, more especially the second-generation reform, in the external sector. In this context, one may hope that the external sector is going to be strong and viable in the years to come.

10

Recent Trends

The latest trends in India's external sector reforms, not covered in the main text, are quite mixed. In some cases, the trend is buoyant. In others, it is not so. Let us have a look at the external sector from different angles during the fiscal year 1999–2000 and beyond.

External Trade

As far as external trade is concerned, the export performance tended to revive from the very beginning of 1999–2000. Value for the year stood at $ 37.556 billion, 13.06 per cent higher than 1998–9 levels. This double-digit growth rate was achieved after a gap of three fiscal years (RBIB, July 2000). Again, during the first quarter of 2000–1, the value of export stood at $ 10.194 billion, 27.65 per cent higher than the figure for the corresponding period of the preceding financial year (*Indian Express*, 2 August 2000).

Buoyancy in export could be explained by the revival of world trade primarily in the wake of economic recovery of the East Asian countries and the rising growth rate of the world economy in general from 2.5 per cent in 1998, to 3.0 per cent in 1999. It is expected to rise to 3.5 per cent during 2000 (*International Capital Markets*, April 2000).

Besides, during this period, the Indian economy experienced low rates of inflation that contributed, along with government incentives, to better export performance. The Union Budget for 1999–2000 offered rationalization and reduction of custom rates, tax benefits to exporters, a liberal foreign cuffency credit scheme and a scheme meant for reducing the transaction cost borne by the exporters. The annual EXIM Policy for 1999–2000 brought in special provisions for export of services, liberal value-addition norms in case of rupee exports and liberal import norms that could boost up exports. The EXIM Policy for 2000–1 aims at decentralization and simplification of the procedures, for example, rationalization of duty drawback scheme and simplification of second-hand capital goods import. The policy proposes establishment of special economic zones that could help augment exports and provides for adherence to the norms of multilateral trade negotiations. To this end, quantitative restrictions related to balance of payments are to be removed rapidly. As many as 714 of 1429 products were freed of quantitative restrictions; the rest are to be brought into OGL list by March 2001. The special import license scheme is to be abolished by March 2001. The export promotion capital goods scheme stands simplified as the threshold limit is removed.

It is a fact that the value of exports did rise, but it did not reduce the trade deficit substantially. The deficit amounted to $ 8.613 billion in 1999–2000 compared to $ 9.170 billion in the preceding financial year. It in fact rose to $ 2.983 billion during the first quarter of 2000, compared to $ 2.369 billion during the corresponding period of 1999–2000 (RBIB, July 2000; *Indian Express*, 2 August 2000). The apparent reason was the higher import growth rate during this period. It moved up from 0.9 per cent during 1998–9 to 8.92 per cent during 1999–2000 and to 27.25 per cent during the first quarter of 2000–1. A high growth rate of imports was mainly because of the rising oil import bill. The growth rate of the oil import bill ascended from –21.7 per cent in 1998–9 to 64.2 per cent during 1999–2000 and it was as high as 92.26 per cent during Apr–June 2000 (*Indian Express*, 2 August 2000). It does not mean that the non-oil import bill did not inflate — it did, but at a much lower rate.

Foreign Direct Investment

As far as FDI is concerned, the policy continued to remain liberal. Also, fresh incentives were given along with greater transparency in the approval system. The approval time for FIPB clearance was reduced to 30 days. The foreign-owned Indian holding companies were allowed to make downstream investments within permissible equity limits without prior approval from FIPB. The Insurance Regulatory Development Act passed by the Parliament in December 1999 permitted foreign equity stake in the insurance sector up to 26 per cent of the total paid-up capital. In February 2000, the coverage of the automatic-route provision of FDI was expanded in a big way. In June 2000, 100 per cent FDI was allowed in certain e-commerce ventures under specified conditions. Power and refining sectors too could avail of 100 per cent foreign equity participation under automatic approval scheme. The dividend balancing requirements for FDI in consumer goods were scrapped and repatriation was allowed without insisting on additional exports (*Economic Times,* 13 June 2000).

It was the continuance of the liberal policy that helped enlarge the number of collaboration agreements. There were 2224 cases of collaborations in 1999 compared to 1786 in 1998. Out of 2224 cases, 1726 were financial collaborations and 498 technical. However, the amount of approved investment was only Rs 283.67 billion compared to Rs 308.14 billion in 1998. Again, during the first half of 2000, there were 1105 collaborations involving Rs 146.4 billion compared to Rs 162.4 billion during the corresponding period of the preceding year (FIPB documents). This way, there was marginal fall in the amount of approved investment during one and a half years ending June 2000.

The year, 1999 witnessed an increase in geographic concentration as far as sources of FDI were concerned. The top four countries, namely, Mauritius, South Korea, USA and the UK accounted for half the approved investment compared to 43 per cent dong 1998. The concentration increased further during the first six months of 2000 as the top four investing countries, namely, Mauritius, USA, Japan and Germany shared 54 per cent of the approved FDI. However, the sectoral concentration decreased during 1999. There was no single sector representing even one-fourth of the total approval, whereas fuel and power alone had accounted for 45 per cent of the approved FDI in 1998.

What is remarkable is that the period covering 1999 and the first half of 2000 witnessed greater implementation of FDI proposals. The actual inflow stood at 59.5 per cent and 63.1 per cent of the approved amount respectively during these two periods compared to only 43.3 per cent in 1998. This is perhaps due to increased political stability and better performance of the Indian economy as well as growing returns on investment. According to a study covering 50 foreign companies operating in India, the rate of return on capital rose from 10.68 per cent during 1998–9 to 13.03 per cent in 1999–2000 (*Economic Times*, 12 June 2000).

Foreign Portfolio Investment

The amount of foreign portfolio investment (net) took a big jump from $ –61 million in 1998–9 to $ 3.026 billion during 1999–2000. The rise was manifest in all the three components, but it was more obvious in the case of FIIs' investment. Their net investment, which was $ –390 million during 1998–9 increased to $ 2.135 billion during 1999–2000, although there were wide variations in the monthly figures (RBIB, July 2000).

Greater net investment could be attributed to economic revival and better health of the stock market as also to encouraging governmental policies. For example, the Government allowed high net-worth individuals to invest through the SEBI-registered FIIs. The domestic fund managers were allowed to manage foreign funds for making investments in Indian capital market. The Budget Proposals for 2000–1 allowed the FIIs to invest up to 40 per cent of the equity shares in a company. This was earlier 24 per cent in general and 30 per cent in specific cases. Again, it is the lower price-earning ratio in the Indian capital market that has attracted FIIs' investment in a considerable measure. It is 14.6 per cent in India compared to over 25 per cent in China and South Korea and as high as 42 per cent in the US (*Economic Times*, 19 May 2000). In this context, it is revealing that the FIIs have of late started showing preference for debt securities.

Their net investment in debt securities rose from a very nominal figure in 1998 and $ 3.5 million in 1999 to $ 10.4 million in January 2000 and to $ 57.5 million during the first 18 days of February 2000 (*Economic Times,* 22 February 2000).

Turning to the second component of foreign portfolio investment, one finds that during 1999–2000, $ 757 million worth of Euro-issues were floated. The actual inflow, also taking into account earlier issues, stood at $ 768 million during this period, which is slightly less than three-fold that during 1998–9. The larger inflow is perhaps due to liberal policies of the govermnent along with revival of the industrial sector. The government has created an automatic route for accessing the international capital market under ADR/GDR mechanism. The Budget Proposals for 2000–1 have permitted raising of such funds without governmental approval if half such proceeds are to be utilized for acquiring companies abroad.

Last but not least, the third component representing transfer of off-shore funds was marked with an inflow of $ 123 million during 1999–2000 compared to only $ 59 million during 1998–9 (RBIB, July 2000).

Non-resident Indians

Detailed figures regarding NRIs' investment are not available, yet those concerning their bank deposits are available for 1999–2000. The figures reveal that there is an increase in their net bank deposit. It was $ 1797 million during 1999–2000 compared to $ 934 million during 1998–9. In case of FCNRB deposits, the net deposit during 1999–2000 was $ 746 million compared to a negative figure during the preceding fiscal year. The size of net NRERA deposits was $ 772 million during 1999–2000, but that of NRNR deposits was only $ 279 million or around half of that during 1998–9 (RBIB, July 2000).

Overseas Investment

India's overseas investment has shown a rising trend. In 1999, 238 WOSs were approved compared to an annual average of

133 during preceding three years. Similarly, 112 approved non-WOS ventures is also larger than 106 which is the annual average of approvals during 1996–8. In fact, the policy in this respect has turned more liberal. In November 1999, the balancing requirements were scrapped and investment in projects with longer gestation lag was allowed. In March 2000, the ceiling for automatic approval was raised from $ 15 million to $ 50 millions The value limit of $ 15 million in respect of fast-track investment out of the EEFC account was also enhanced to $ 50 million. The companies operatmg in the area of information technology were permitted to acquire business up to $ 100 million abroad through stock swap subject to specific guidelines. However, the impact of this latest move is yet to be seen.

At the end of September 1999, for which the figures are available, there were 831 active WOSs involving $ 1368 million of investment, out of which 275 were in operation and the rest were under various stages of implementation. It is revealed that 64 per cent of the ventures had moved only to four countries, namely, USA, UK, Singapore and Mauritius. This shows a high degree of geographic concentration. This is not all. The sectoral concentration was still higher with approximately 90 per cent of the ventures in non-financial services alone. As regards the contribution of the WOSs to the balance of payments, one finds that the cumulative amount of foreign exchange earnings on account of dividend, fees and export in respect of these ventures stood at Rs 14.907 billion at the end of September 1999 (GOI, 2000a).

Similarly, there were 912 active non-WOS ventures abroad involving an investment of $ 1150.32 million at the end of September 1999. As many as 392 were in operation leaving the rest under different stages of implementation. Geographic/ sectoral concentration was not so high as in case of WOSs with only one-third ventures in the top four countries on the list, USA, UK, UAE and Sri Lanka; and nearly one-third ventures in non-financial services. The cumulative inflow of foreign exchange on account of dividend, fees and export earnings amounted to Rs. 17.351 billion up to September 1999 (GOI, 2000a).

External Debt

The trend towards increasing external debt burden that was evident during 1998-9, continued as the total debt jumped up from $ 97.677 billion at the end of March 1999 to $ 99.005 billion at the end of December 1999 (CMIE, July 2000). But since there was a fall in the debt burden in respect of commercial borrowings (ECBs), the policy regarding external commercial borrowing got liberal during 1999-2000. Companies and financial institutions were allowed to raise ECBs up to $ 5 million for a three-year maturity. Foreign exchange earners, such as exporters, etc. and the infrastructure project companies were given a still bigger hand to go for ECBs. The maturity structure was rationalized. The borrowers could park the proceeds abroad subject to monitoring by the RBI. Pre-payment facilities were provided under specific conditions. Area for the utilization of ECBs was expanded, the approval formalities eased. In June 2000, a few more relaxations were made. They raised the new ECB approval limit up to $ 50 million. The refinancing companies were allowed to utilize the credit enhancement scheme under specific conditions. The RBI was given some additional powers concerning sanction and pre-payment. The Government fixed ECB ceiling of $ 8.5 billion for the fiscal year 2000-1 with a view to maintaining a balance between liberalization of borrowing on one hand and a check on the growth of debt burden, on the other.

BOP at a Glance

The recent developments in the external sector could well be reflected in the balance of payments statement. Statistics reveal a 29.1 per cent increase in the trade deficit (on BOP account) during 1999-2000, however, this big gap was largely bridged by net inflow on invisible account. As a result, the current account deficit during 1999-2000 increased only by 3.1 per cent over the preceding fiscal year. In absolute terms, the current account deficit was $ 4163 million compared to $ 4038 million during 1998-9.

Again, the inflow on capital account was larger than the current account deficit. The excess inflow over and above the current account deficit added to the foreign exchange reserve that stood at $ 38.036 billion at the end of March 2000.

Analysing the capital account transactions, it is found that the size of inflow (net) on account of loans during 1999–2000 was lower at $ 1601 million compared to $ 4418 million during, 1998–9. This was mainly because of drastic fall in net commercial borrowings from $ 4367 million during 1998–9 to barely $ 333 million during 1999–2000. On the contrary, there was greater inflow of foreign investment — direct and portfolio. It was $ 5117 million compared to $ 2312 million during 1998–9. Moreover, the net inflow on account of banking transactions, stood at $ 2727 million in 1999–2000 compared to $ 1480 million during 1998–9 (RBIB, July 2000).

Moving Closer to CAC

In view of greater ease in the overall balance of payments position, the Indian government took a few further steps towards CAC during 1999–2000. To mention the more important of them, ADs were allowed to provide foreign exchange cover to FIIs up to 15 per cent of their outstanding equity investment. The foreign office of the export houses came to avail of specific facilities from foreign banks. The Indian entities were allowed to hedge exposure to bullion prices arising from export commitments in London Bullion Market or in recognized international exchanges. The Indian companies can now use commercial papers for borrowing from overseas corporate bodies (OCBs) on non-repairable terms and subject to specific conditions. The banks accepting gold under Gold Deposit Scheme can use exchange traded/over-the-counter hedging products in order to minimize risk. The shares of Indian companies can be sold/purchased among NRIs/OCBs. The individuals, such as tourists, etc. can hedge their foreign exchange exposure through ADs. These are some of the major steps. Others may follow if the balance of payments position improves further in future.

Appendix

A Note on Capital-account Convertibility

The term, capital-account convertibility (CAC) means relaxing controls on capital-account transactions. In the process of external sector reforms that witnesses *inter alia* transition from a controlled regime to a market-determined one, CAC is one of the steps in the concluding phase. After attainment of full convertibility on current account transactions by August 1994, there was a long debate on whether and how to go for CAC. The RBI appointed a committee under the chairmanship of S. S. Tarapore in February 1997 to explore this and suggest necessary measures. The Committee's report in June 1997 suggested among other things how to phase on to the CAC and what pre-conditions were necessary for its smooth operation (RBI, 1997a). Some of the recommendations were acted upon. Several were not implemented due to unwarranted changes in macroeconomic variables in general and external-sector variables in particular, since late 1997. It is thus very relevant to discuss here the steps taken in this context against the backdrop of Tarapore Committee recommendations and whether the economy is in a position to undertake further steps towards CAC.

Rationale for CAC

Countries with tenuous foreign-exchange reserves and weak balance of payments position often apply controls on capital-account transactions which, however, become ineffective in the long run. Capital inflows and outflows begin taking place through illegal channels distorting the economic structure. Mathieson and Rojas-Suarez (1993) have examined the efficacy of control on capital-account transactions based on the experiences of some of the developed and the developing countries and have found that it is often ineffective. In fact, it is the growing difficulties in enforcing capital control that have led Quirk and Evans (1995) and Cooper (1998) to argue for capital-account liberalization.

In the process of capital-account liberalization, the capital-account transactions are made independent of day-to-day approval of the monetary authorities. The entire episode is left to the market forces — the financial market of the country gets integrated with the foreign financial markets and the economy is able to avail of large amount of external resources. As a result, the process of economic growth is stimulated.

Again, there is greater freedom for individual decision-making as to how to get necessary resources and how to use the excess reserves. The residents are able to hold an internationally diversified portfolio of assets which lessens the risks in investment and augments the risk-adjusted return on capital. Since the resources are allocated internationally on the basis of supply of, and demand for, funds, the allocation is optimal maximizing the welfare gains. Although all this is possible only when the financial market is 'efficient' and, at the same time, there are no domestic distortions (Eichengreen and Mussa, 1998).

Tarapore Committee Recommendations

Framework of Recommendations

Even before the Tarapore Committee report was tabled, there had been limited relaxation of certain capital-account transactions, such as direct and portfolio investment and non-resident deposits. The Committee ruled out abrupt introduction of any further relaxation and spanned the process over three annual phases beginning 1997–8. The relaxation concerned transactions on account of individuals, banking and non-banking financial companies, non-financial companies and the financial market in general. We present here some of the major recommendations of the Committee.

The Committee recommended to allowing resident *individuals* to make foreign-currency-denominated deposits with a bank in India, to borrow from non-residents at an interest rate not exceeding London Inter-bank Offer Rate (LIBOR) and to transfer financial capital abroad for opening bank accounts. It also allowed non-resident individuals to transfer capital from non-repatriable assets held in India. The individuals making foreign direct/portfolio investments/ disinvestment were not required to get RBI permission. There was, of course, a ceiling with respect to the amount in all these cases but it gradually increased in successive phases.

Indian companies were allowed to issue foreign-currency-denominated bonds to residents, to invest in foreign-currency-denominated bonds, to transfer financial capital abroad for the purpose of opening bank accounts and to have entire export earnings in the form of foreign currency without seeking permission from the RBI. The non-resident companies were allowed to make investments or disinvestments in and out of India without seeking permission from the RBI.

As regards *banks*, the Committee recommended enhancing the limit of Indian bank borrowing from then existing level of $ 10 million to 50 per cent of their unimpaired Tier I capital in the first year, to 100 per cent of such capital in the final year. As per the Committee's recommendations, bank investment could go up to 75 per cent of their time and demand liabilities in India. They did not have to seek RBI permission for making buyers' credit and for accepting deposits and making loans in foreign currency. The non-resident banks that were using their rupee account only for merchant-based transactions were allowed to make investment within a limited range.

The *non-banking financial companies* (*NBFC*) were allowed to make investment abroad subject to specified ceiling. The non-resident NBFCs were not required to seek approval of the RBI for their portfolio investment in India within the 30 per cent ceiling provided by the Government.

The Committee recommended necessary changes in the *financial market*. For liberal provisions it suggested the forward cover in the foreign-exchange market and allowed NBFCs to function as authorized dealers (AD). It permitted the transaction of derivatives and allowed the participants in the foreign-exchange market to approach the foreign derivatives market on their own and not necessarily through the ADs.

In the case of the *money market*, the Committee recommended deregulation of deposit rates, allowing FIIs to operate in the treasury bill/government securities market, and setting up of a public debt office to look after the primary issue of dated securities and treasury bills that could ease the burden of the RBI.

As regards the *import of gold*, the Committee brought in the ambit of canalizing agency those banks and financial institutions that could operate freely in the domestic and international gold market. It allowed banks to offer gold-denominated deposits and loans and to provide working capital gold loans to jewellery makers. It also recommended gold derivatives including forward trading in which both residents and non-residents can operate.

Pre-conditions

The Tarapore Committee was aware of the pre-conditions necessary for phasing on to the CAC. They were very concerned with the fiscal consolidation, a mandated inflation target, strength of the financial and banking sectors and the balance of payments situation.

Fiscal performance is mirrored by the size of the fiscal deficit. Hence, the Committee relied on the size of gross fiscal deficit that should come down to 3.5 per cent of GDP by 1999-2000. For this downtrend, the Committee emphasized on the reduction of interest burden on domestic debt and on the improvement in the fiscal position of different states.

As regards inflation, the Committee was of the view that the Parliament should target a medium-term inflation scenario averaging between 3 and 5 per cent. RBI should have the freedom of operation within this targeted mandate.

Again, the Committee made several suggestions to revamp the banking and financial sectors. For example, it was of the opinion that banks should be rationalized so as to conform to international standards, the reserve requirements should also include non-resident liabilities and come down to 3 per cent, the ratio of non-performing assets should come down to 5 per cent, the interest should be completely deregulated and the financial institutions and the NBFCs should be well-equipped to face any risk on account of volatility in exchange rates and interest rates. The Committee stressed on exchange-rate stability in view of the fact that both appreciation and depreciation of the rupee are harmful for the smooth functioning of the CAC. It, therefore, suggested the establishment of a neutral real effective exchange rate (REER) by the RBI which could fluctuate within a band of +/- 5 per cent. The RBI should review the REER periodically against the backdrop of changes in macroeconomic fundamentals and also intervene, if necessary.

Finally, the balance of payments position should be strong enough to sustain any large outflow of foreign exchange. The Committee was of the view that the ratio of current account receipts to GDP should rise from then existing 15 per cent and that the foreign-exchange reserves should be comfortable so as to sustain temporary cyclical changes and shocks leading to sudden outflow of foreign exchange. Taking into account the volatility in current account and capital-account outflows, the Committee laid down four guidelines: (i) reserves should not be less than six-months' import bill; (ii) they should be able to finance three-months' import bill and at the same time one half of annual debt-service charges; (iii) the short-term debt and portfolio stock to reserves ratio should be within 60 per cent; and (iv) the foreign-exchange assets to currency ratio should be maintained at 70 per cent.

Implementation of the Recommendations

As per the recommendations of Tarapore Committee, the RBI allowed the ADs to hedge overseas loan exposure for their clients through swap and forward covers and to repatriate money arising out of non-repatriable deposits of NRIs and overseas corporate bodies without prior approval. The FIIs were also given forward cover with respect to their investment in debt, at its current value and not exceeding the maturity.

In October 1997, the Government decided to allow free import of gold by eight banks and three canalizing agencies. As per the monetary policy pronouncements, the exporters were allowed to retain one-half of the foreign-exchange earnings in EEFC account which was only one-quarter earlier. This was 100 per cent in the case of completely EOUs and the EPZs. The exporters could sell forward the balance in their EEFC account, although they were to abide by the rule that dollars sold forward must be meant for delivery. Foreign banks, too, could hedge their repatriable profits. Earlier they used to get such permission on a case by case basis.

Indian export projects did not require prior approval of the RBI and companies were allowed to open their offices abroad. Current and capital expenditure of those offices were allowed up to their foreign-exchange earnings. Banks could extend credit/non-credit facilities to Indian ventures operating abroad up to 5 per cent of their unimpaired Tier I capital and could undertake forfeiting of medium-term export receivables which was earlier the domain of the EXIM Bank. Again, the SEBI-registered Indian funds managers including mutual funds were allowed to invest in overseas market within specific limits.

In the first week of November 1997, the RBI identified three broad areas for taking steps towards CAC. First, in the money market, the RBI proposed to reduce the minimum period of term deposits, to reduce the lock-in period of mutual funds, to enlarge the participation in repo market, to scrap inter-bank liabilities from statutory liquidity ratio and cash reserves ratio requirements and to introduce intermediaries in the money market. It also planned to increase the number of primary dealers and enhance their underwriting power, to allow the FIIs to invest in treasury bills and to introduce interest rate futures in treasury bills and dated government securities. Next it proposed to permit the issuance of foreign-currency-denominated bonds to the residents, to allow the FIIs to hedge the equity exposures in the forward market, to allow financial institutions to act as ADs in foreign-exchange market and to introduce derivatives.

However, soon thereafter, with the deepening of the impact of South-East Asian crisis on India's external sector, the Indian Government adopted a go-slow policy. It learnt a lesson from the experiences of the South-East Asian countries where the economy had registered a high growth rate without warranted strength built up in the financial sector. It thus preferred to take any step towards CAC only after desired improvement in the pre-conditions. Moreover, there were many factors at play, apart from the South-East Asian crisis, that led to poor export performance, lower inflow of foreign direct and portfolio investment, to growing fiscal deficit and to rising external debt during 1998–9. Nevertheless, a few steps were taken in 1998–9. The RBI allowed the branches of foreign companies to remit profits to their head offices through ADs without prior approval. ADs were permitted to provide the forward cover facility to FIIs with regard to fresh investments in India in equity and also for appreciation in the market value of their investment to a specified limit. The same facility was extended to NRIs/OCBs for their portfolio investments. ADs were also allowed to reimburse credit cards organizations in certain cases up to a specified limit and to make remittances related to registration of patents and trade marks with any foreign authorities. The EEFC account holders were permitted to use funds in the account for making bonafide payments in foreign exchange abroad related to their trade or overseas investment under specific conditions. Indian entities having genuine underlying exposures were allowed to access international commodity exchanges for exchange traded futures and options purchase. Foreign embassies, missions, and diplomats, were permitted to open foreign-currency accounts with any AD in India without the approval of the RBI but subject to certain conditions. The RBI announced a package of reforms in the banking sector in conformity with the recommendations of the Second Narsimham Committee report of 1998, that could pave the way for CAC.

Sustainability of the Economy for CAC

Was the economy in a position to sustain CAC at the end of 1998–9 or during the early months of 1999-2000? The answer may not be very difficult in view of the availability of statistics pertaining to the Indian economy at this very juncture. Table A1.1 presents some of the more relevant statistics against the backdrop of the preconditions suggested by the Tarapore Committee. Some of the macroeconomic fundamentals are

Table A1.1   Macroeconomic Variables Influencing CAC Decision

Macroeconomic variables	Actuals during 1998–9/March 1999-end	Tarapore Committee norms during 1997–2000
1. Gross fiscal deficit of Centre and State Governments during 1998–9 as % of GDP	8.5	3.5 or less by 1999–2000
2. Inflation rate at the end of March 1999	4.8%	3–5%
3. Non-performing assets as % of banks' net advances at the end of March 1999	7.5	5.0 or less
4. Foreign-currency assets/currency ratio at the end of March 1999	74%	70% or above
5. Foreign-exchange reserves to cover import during 1998–9	8.3 months	6 months or above
6. Foreign-exchange reserves/ 3-month import + one-half of debt-service charges during 1998–9	205%	100% or above
7. Current account receipts/GDP ratio during 1998–9	14.3%	15% or above
8. Fluctuation band of REER during 1998–9	Monthly variation+/– 5% in index between 103.88 and 95.86 (100 = 1993-94)	
9. Short-term debt + portfolio stock/foreign-exchange reserves ratio at the end of March 1999	60.93 %	60 % or less

Sources: 1. RBI, (1999) *Annual Report* 1998–9, Bombay.
2. RBI, (1999) *Report on Trend and Progress of Banking in India: 1998–9*, Bombay.
3. RBI, (1997) *Report of the Committee on Capital Account Convertibility (Tarapore Committee Report)*, Bombay.

operating in favour of moving on to the CAC, but the others are not. Again, in some cases, the difference between the actuals and the norms is large, whereas in others, it is only marginal. For example, the rate of inflation, the foreign-currency asset to currency ratio, the foreign-exchange reserves coverage of the imports and the foreign-exchange reserves coverage of the imports and external debt-service charges indicate that the government may go for CAC. On the other hand, the gross fiscal deficit to GDP ratio, non-performing assets ratio of the banks, current receipts to GDP ratio, short-term debt and portfolio stock to foreign-exchange reserves ratio and the degree of volatility in REER do not support any move towards CAC. Again, the inflation rate, current account receipts to GDP ratio and the short-term debt and portfolio stock to foreign-exchange reserves ratio are at the margin. They may fluctuate any time and influence the decision accordingly. Thus it would be proper to suggest that the government should be very careful of taking forward any step in this context. However, if the economy performs better in the future and if the performance is firm and does not seem reversible, the Government can think in terms of CAC.

Bibliography

Avramovic, D., et al (1964), *Economic Growth and External Debt*, Baltimore, John Hopkins Press.

Balassa, B. (1981), *Structural Adjustment Policies in Developing Economies*, World Bank working staff paper No. 464, Washington, DC.

Bauer, P. (1961), 'Import Capacity and Economic Development', *Economic Journal*, 71(2), pp. 442–6.

Bhagwati, J. (1998), 'The Design of Indian Development' in Ahluwalia, I.J. and I.M.D. Little (eds.), *India's Economic Reforms and Development*, Delhi: Oxford University Press, p. 36.

Bhagwati, J. (1970), 'Tying of Aid' in J. Bhagwati and R.S. Eckaus (eds.), *Foreign Aid*, Harmondoworth Middlesex: Penguin series, pp. 235–93.

Bhattacharya, B. (1994), *Policy Impediments to Foreign Direct Investment in India*, New Delhi: Indian Institute of Foreign Trade.

Brahmbhatta, M. *et al.* (1996), *India in the Global Economy*, Washington, DC: The World Bank.

Business Standard (New Delhi), 17 January 1998.

—— 6 April 1998.

—— 23 May 1998.

Centre for Monitoring Indian Economy (1998), *Monthly Review of the Economy*, Bombay, March issue.

—— (2000), *Monthly Review of the Economy*, July issue.

Chimni, B.S. (1999), 'India and Ongoing Review of WTO Dispute Settlement System', *Economic and Political Weekly*, Jan 30-Feb 5, pp. 264-7.

Chisti, S. and S.K. Upadhyay (1981), 'Impact of Oil Price Hike on Terms of Trade and Balance of Payments', *Foreign Trade Review*, 16(2), pp. 101-26.

Cooper, R.N. (1998), 'Should Capital-Account Convertibility be a World Objective?' in Kenen, P.B. (ed.), *Should the IMF Pursue Capital-Account Convertibility*, Essays in International Finance no. 207, Princeton: Princeton University Press.

Dhar B. and S.S. Roy (1999), 'Strengthening the External Sector', *Economic and Political Weekly*, July 18-24, pp. 2020-3.

Economic Times (New Delhi), 12 May 1994.

—— 14 October 1994.

—— 19 May 1999.

—— 22 February 2000.

—— 12 June 2000.

—— 13 June 2000.

Eichengreen, B. and Michael Mussa (1998), *Capital Account Liberalisation: Theoretical and Practical Aspects*, IMF Occasional Paper no. 172, Washington, DC: International Monetary Fund.

Encarnation, Dennis G. (1989), *Dislodging Multinationals: India's Strategy in Comparative Perspective*, Ithaca and London: Cornell University Press, p. 70.

Foreign Investment Promotion Board (1998), *Select Documents*, New Delhi, Ministry of Industry, Government of India.

—— (2000), *Select Documents*, Ministry of Industry, Government of India.

Ghemawat, P. and M. Patibandla (1999), 'India's Exports since the Reforms: Three Analytic Industry Studies' in Jeffrey D. Sachs, Ashutosh Varshney and Nirupam Bajpai (eds), *India in the Era of Economic Reforms*, New Delhi: Oxford University Press.

Government of India (1992), *Economic Survey 1991-2*, New Delhi: Ministry of Finance.

—— (1993), *Economic Survey 1992-3*, New Delhi: Ministry of Finance.

—— (1994), *Economic Survey 1993–4*, New Delhi: Ministry of Finance.

—— (1997), *Economic Survey 1996–7*, New Delhi: Ministry of Finance.

—— (1998), *Economic Survey 1997–8*, New Delhi: Ministry of Finance.

—— (1999a), *Budget for 1999-2000: Speech of the Minister of Finance*, New Delhi.

—— (1999b), *Economic Survey 1998–9*, New Delhi: Ministry of Finance.

—— (2000), *Economic Survey 1999–2000*, New Delhi: Ministry of Finance.

—— (2000a), *Annual Report of the Ministry of Commerce and Industry: 1999–2000*, New Delhi.

Gupta, S.P. (1998), *Post-Reform India: Emerging Trends*, New Delhi: Allied Publishers.

Hirsch, F and I. Higgins (1970), 'An Indicator of Effective Exchange Rates', *IMF Staff Papers*, 17(3), pp. 453–87.

Hood N. and S. Young (1979), *The Economics of Multinational Enterprise*, London: Longman.

Hymer, S.H. (1976), *The International Operations of National Firms: A Study of Direct Investment*, Cambridge Mass: MIT Press.

Indian Express (New Delhi), 2 August 2000.

Indian Investment Centre (1997), *Investment Opportunities Available to Non-Resident Indians*, New Delhi.

Indian Investment Centre (1991), *Monthly Newsletter*, New Delhi, various issues.

—— (1997a), *Foreign Investment Policy of the Government of India*, New Delhi.

—— (1997b) *Investment Opportunities Available to Non-resident Indians*, New Delhi.

—— (1998), *Monthly Newsletter*, New Delhi, February issue.

Indian Investment Centre (1998a), *Joint-ventures and Wholly-owned Subsidiaries Abroad*, New Delhi.

Inter-Economics (1992), September p. 251.

International Capital Markets (2000), April issue.

International Finance Corporation (1993), *Emerging Stock Markets Fact-book*, Washington DC.

Jalan, B. (1991), *India's Economic Crisis: The Way Ahead*, Delhi: Oxford University Press.

Joshi, K. and D'souza, D. (1999), 'Wanted, An India Brand Manager for FDI', *The Economic Times*, 26 February.

Krueger, A. (1961), 'Export Prospects and Economic Growth: India—A Comment', *Economic Journal*, LXXI.

Kundra, A. (2000), *The Performance of India's Export Zones: A Comparision with Chinese Approach*, New Delhi: Sage Publishers.

Lall, S. (1982), 'The Emergence of Third World Multinationals: Indian Joint-ventures Overseas', *World Development*, 10(1), pp. 127–46.

Massell, B.F. (1970), 'Export Instability and Economic Structure', *American Economic Review*, 60(4), pp. 619–30.

Mathieson, D.J. and L. Rojas-Suarez (1993), *Liberalisation of the Capital Account: Experiences and Issues*, IMF Occasional Paper no. 103, Washington, DC: International Monetary Fund.

Meric I and C. Meric (1989), 'Potential Gains from International Portfolio Diversification and Intertemporal Stability from Seasonality in International Stock Market Relationship', *Journal of Banking and Finance*, 13(4), pp. 627–40.

Ohlin, G. (1966), *Aid and Indebtedness*, Paris, OECD.

—— (1966a), *Foreign Aid Policies Reconsidered*, Paris, OECD, pp. 13–51.

Patel, S.J. (1959), 'Export prospects and Economic Growth—India', *Economic Journal*, 69(3), pp. 490–506.

Quirk, P. and O. Evans (1995), *Capital Account Convertibility: Review of Experience and Implications for IMF Policies*, IMF Occasional Paper no. 131, Washington DC: International Monetary Fund.

Rangarajan, C. (1990), 'The Balance of Payments Scenario', *Seventh G.L. Mehta Memorial Lecture*, Bombay: IIT.

Reilly, W. (1987), 'Management and Training for Development: The Hombe Thesis', *Public Administration and Development*, 7(1), pp. 25–42.

Reserve Bank of India (1996), *Facilities for Non-Resident Indians*, Bombay.

—— (1997), *Report on Currency and Finance 1996–7*, Bombay.

—— (1997a), *Report of the Committee on Capital Account Convertibility*, Bombay.

—— (1999), *Annual Report: 1998–9*, Bombay.

Reserve Bank of India Bulletin, (1998), July issue.

—— (1999), various issues.

—— (2000), July issue.

Rhomberg, R.R. (1976), 'Indices of Effective Exchange Rates', *IMF Staff Papers*, 23(1), pp. 88–112.

Rodriguez, C.A. (1989), *Macroeconomic Policies for Structural Adjustment*, Washington, DC, The World Bank.

Rosenbaum, H.J. and W.G. Tyler (1975), 'South-South Relations: The Economic and Political Content of Interactions among Developing Countries' in Bergsten, C.F. and L.B. Krause (eds.), *World Politics and International Economics*, Washington DC: Brookings Institute.

Sharan, Vyuptakesh (1968), *Role of Foreign Capital in Indian Economic Development* since 1951, doctoral dissertation, Patna University.

—— (1968), 'Foreign Investments in India: Trends, Problems and Prospect', *Foreign Trade Review*, 27(1), pp. 74–84.

—— (1975), 'Foreign Aid and Economic Development: An Indian Experience', *Journal of Social and Economic Studies*, 7(1), pp. 129–49.

—— (1985), 'Internationalism of Third World Firms: An Indian Case Study', *International Marketing Review*, 2 (Summer), pp. 63–71.

—— (1991), *The World Bank Group and the SAARC Nations*, New Delhi, Anmol Publications.

—— (1993), 'Foreign Investment in India: Role of Non-Resident Indians', *Economia Internazionale*, 46(1), pp. 43–56.

—— (1998), 'Recent Trends in Foreign Direct Investment in India', *International Capital Markets*, 18(4), pp. 29–34.

Shrivastawa, A. (1997), 'Portfolio Investment in Developing Countries', *International Capital Markets*, 17(4), pp. 36–42.

Srinivasan, T.N. (1998), 'India's Export Performance: A Comparative Analysis' in I.J. Ahluwalia, and I.M.D. Little (eds.), *India's Economic Reforms and Development*, Delhi: Oxford University Press.

Taylor, L. (1988), *Varieties of Stabilization Experience: Towards Sensible Macroeconomics in the Third World*, Oxford: Clarendon Press.

The Statesman (Calcutta), 14 December 1955.

The World Bank (1980), *Annual Report 1980*, Washington, DC, p. 19.

—— (1990), *World Debt Tables*, Washington, DC.

—— (1998), *India 1998: Macroeconomic Update*, Washington, DC.

—— (1999), *Global Development Finance*, Washington, DC, Part I.

Ting, Wenlee (1982), 'The Product Development Process in NIC Multinational', *Columbia Journal of World Business*, 17(1), pp. 76–81.

United Nations (1998), *World Investment Report 1998: Trends and Determinants*, New York and Geneva: UNCTAD.

—— (1999), *World Investment Report 1999: Foreign Direct Investment and the Challenge of Development*, New York and Geneva: UNCTAD.

Vernon, R. (1966), 'International Investment and International Trade in the Product Cycle', *Quarterly Journal of Economics*, 80(2), pp. 190–207.

—— (1979), 'The Product Cycle Hypothesis in a New International Environment' *Oxford Bulletin of Economics and Statistics*, 41(4), pp. 255–67.

Wells, L.T. Jr. (1969), 'Test of Product Life Cycle Model of International Trade, *Quarterly Journal of Economics*, 83(1), pp. 152–62.

Wheeler, D. and A. Mody (1992), 'International Investment Location Decisions', *Journal of International Economics*, 33(1 & 2), pp. 57–76.

Woodward, D. (1992) *Debt, Adjustment and Poverty in Developing Countries*, London, Pinter Publishers, Part II, pp. 169–95.